AESTHETICS AND MORALITY

Continuum Aesthetics

Series Editor: Derek Matravers, Open University and University of Cambridge, UK

The Continuum Aesthetics Series looks at the aesthetic questions and issues raised by all major art forms. Stimulating, engaging and accessible, the series offers food for thought not only for students of aesthetics, but also for anyone with an interest in philosophy and the arts.

Titles available from Continuum:

Aesthetics and Architecture, Edward Winters
Aesthetics and Literature, David Davies
Aesthetics and Morality, Elisabeth Schellekens
Aesthetics and Music, Andy Hamilton

Forthcoming in 2008:
Aesthetics and Film, Katherine Thomson
Aesthetics and Nature, Glenn Parsons
Aesthetics and Painting, Jason Gaiger

AESTHETICS AND MORALITY

ELISABETH SCHELLEKENS

continuum

Continuum International Publishing Group

The Tower Building, 11 York Road, London SE1 7NX
80 Maiden Lane, Suite 704, New York NY 10038

www.continuumbooks.com

First published 2007

British Library Cataloguing-in-Publication Data
A catalogue record for this book is available from the British Library.

ISBN-10: HB: 0-8264-8524-3
PB: 0-8264-9762-4
ISBN-13: HB: 978-0-8264-8524-3
PB: 978-0-8264-9762-8

Library of Congress Cataloging-in-Publication Data

Schellekens, Elisabeth.
Aesthetics and morality / Elisabeth Schellekens.
p. cm.
Includes bibliographical references and index.
ISBN-13: 978-0-8264-8524-3
ISBN-13: 978-0-8264-9762-8
1. Aesthetics. 2. Ethics. I. Title.
BH39.S3285 2008
111'.85--dc22

2007019576

Typeset by Kenneth Burnley, Wirral, Cheshire
Printed and bound in Great Britain by Cromwell Press Ltd, Trowbridge, Wiltshire

CONTENTS

ACKNOWLEDGEMENTS

Philosophical Aesthetics and Moral Philosophy are areas of investigation that have fascinated me ever since my days as a student, and to all intents and purposes, long before that too. Many people, both philosophers and non-philosophers, have provided me with food for thought and shaped my reflections on the questions raised in these fields over the years, often in ways that I am no longer even aware of. In particular, though, I would like to express my heartfelt gratitude to Ronald Hepburn, who first taught me Aesthetics and Moral Philosophy at the University of Edinburgh and who opened my eyes to the richness and depth of these spheres of enquiry.

I would like to thank Sarah Campbell and her colleagues from Continuum Press for their help and enthusiasm for the project. I am grateful to Derek Matravers, the Series Editor, for many interesting conversations and exchanges on the subject. Also, Ella Carpenter and Catherine Harris, who with their great friendship have sustained and encouraged me throughout, and Matthew Murphy, for the many excellent examples of immoral art. I am particularly grateful to my family, who have taught me to see the value of beauty and goodness, and encouraged me to pursue them at all levels of life.

Finally, I would like to thank Guy Dammann who read the manuscript with infinite care and in minute detail, and without whose analytic yet sensitive understanding of the material this book would most definitively be an inferior version of itself. Without Guy, there would simply be neither beauty nor goodness in my world, and thus most probably no book to speak of.

INTRODUCTION

I

Philosophical Aesthetics is a discipline with fewer natural friends than foes. From within the academic world, it is regularly considered ancillary, charged with dealing merely with 'soft' issues. Aesthetics, it is held, is hardly concerned with the central questions of Philosophy, such as how we acquire knowledge of how the world and its contents are to be divided, and thus fails to address those areas of investigation held to be of genuine importance. Conversely, from outside the academic environment, Aesthetics is often considered either irrelevant or misleading. For philosophical examination of everyday aesthetic phenomena, such as the experience of beauty or the making of an aesthetic judgement, may seem unwarranted and uncalled for. Surely, one may say, the aesthetic is all about the pleasure we stand to gain, the emotive experience we may have, or the general well-being it may bring about? Applying rigorous philosophical method to such notions can only make them dry, dreary and perhaps even unrecognizable.

The overriding aim of this book is to show that the two ways of viewing Aesthetics sketched above are both deeply misguided. In a first instance, academic philosophers who are inclined to hold a negative view of the concerns of Aesthetics are wrong to assume that the discipline does not deal with notions that are pivotal to philosophical analysis and interests in general. On the contrary, Aesthetics engages directly with issues central to Metaphysics, to the theory of knowledge (or Epistemology), and the Philosophy of mind. Although it is certainly true that such investigations are primarily directed at the study of *aesthetic* qualities, *aesthetic* perception and *aesthetic* judgement – and can to that extent be said to target a relatively small and exceptional category – exactly the same questions apply. Further, we can nearly always learn something about the more conventional cases from looking at these slightly unorthodox ones with which they are contrasted.

The approach that will be adopted in this book is in line with this proposed way of casting the questions of Aesthetics in two respects. First, the way in which we shall reflect upon aesthetic matters will mainly be in terms of these wider metaphysical and epistemological issues. Second, it will be assumed that even if not all the concerns that fall within the remit of Aesthetics are specifically metaphysical or epistemological in character, we must begin any thorough enquiry into Aesthetics and the concepts at its heart by addressing these questions, for it is only once progress has been made at this level that we may hope to find genuine and lasting solutions to most of the other, perhaps less far-reaching, concerns.

In a second instance, non-philosophers who adhere to a more or less hostile approach to Aesthetics are profoundly misguided: to think that philosophical scrutiny cannot add anything of substance to the actual everyday phenomena in question reveals a flawed interpretation of the matter. For once we have a clearer idea of the concepts and qualities constitutive of those very phenomena, our experience of them will prove considerably richer and more rewarding than our pre-philosophical ones.

This is not to say, of course, that aesthetic phenomena should not be conceived as fundamentally experiential. Indeed, as is apparent from the first text in which the term 'aesthetics' is used in the way in which we employ it today, namely Alexander Baumgarten's *Aesthetica* of 1750, the notion reveals a typically sensory and affective origin. Clearly, then, aesthetic phenomena have a special relation to their 'lived' character. Nonetheless, examining this character and our experience of it with the help of philosophical resources can only render us more perceptive to detail, more sensitive to the interactions between various features, and more appreciative of the object's aesthetic value.

Philosophical Aesthetics is thus the key to not only an adequate theoretical understanding of aesthetic value and the phenomena derived from it, but also to a more satisfying and worthwhile aesthetic life. The discipline is, then, neither peripheral nor extraneous – as we shall see, it brings to our attention some of the most fundamental questions of Philosophy in a way that has a direct bearing on our everyday experience.

One of the ways in which it is particularly obvious that Aesthetics – or, more specifically, questions about aesthetic value – is in reality far from tangential, philosophically speaking, is in its relation to another kind of value, namely moral value. On the one hand, the relation between aesthetic and moral value targets one of the most important fields open to philosophical investigation in virtue of involving a subject that holds a very significant place in our reflections: concerns about what kind of person one wants to be, what goals one should aspire to, and how one should treat other persons, all form part of Moral Philosophy, and any relation it may bear to another branch of learning that affects or is affected by it deserves our serious attention. On the other hand, the notions of aesthetic and moral value and the interactions between them actually address a set of concerns that, in a sense, may be seen to constitute a philosophical domain of its own. The relation between the aesthetic and the moral acquires a specific philosophical character in this way precisely by urging us to consider traditional philosophical issues from a particularly challenging perspective.

Conceived more broadly, then, Aesthetics and Morality present us with two investigative contexts which are not only interesting in their own right, but also gain a more general importance through presenting us with what may be thought of as a further – and perhaps to a certain extent independent – domain of enquiry. That is to say, embarking on a philosophical examination of the relation between Aesthetics and Morality does not merely amount to investigating Aesthetics and Morality respectively, and drawing certain conclusions about their interactions. Rather, it is the relation itself that is the focus of our study, and the manner in which its two main protagonists enter into one another's philo-sophical territory, so to speak.

In setting out to examine the relation between Aesthetics and Morality, let us not have any false hopes or expectations with regards to the outcome that such an enquiry may yield. For although certain suggestions will be shown to reveal something particularly pressing or something especially important, no direct answers or formulaic solutions will be offered, no question will be definitively settled, and no specific theory will be presented as true in this book. Rather, its main aim is to help the reader see where the theoretical worries lie, what exactly the philosophical questions are, and what the ramifications of these challenges amount to. That is to say, the ambition of this book is to make us all think, and think deeply, about the relation between Aesthetics and Morality in its various forms and under its many guises.

II

Part I, or the two opening chapters of this book, is mainly concerned with the question of whether, and if so how, it is possible to establish where the limits of the aesthetic realm are to be drawn in a twofold attempt to, first, get a better understanding of our subject-matter, so as to, second, disentangle it from the domain of the moral. For on reflection, it is not obvious where the boundaries of the distinctively aesthetic lie, or indeed that there are any such boundaries at all. The question is particularly pertinent in relation to the moral sphere in virtue of some at least seemingly overlapping concerns about value in general. For that reason, the overall aim of Part I is to bring to the fore a concern about whether – and if so to what extent – the aesthetic and the moral infringe upon one another *qua* areas of philosophical enquiry. Where, we will thus ask, does the domain of the aesthetic end and that of the moral begin (or vice versa)? To delimit the aesthetic from the moral is, in other words, a philosophical task in itself, and as such calls for our attention from the very beginning of our investigation.

In Chapter 1, it is the notion of aesthetic experience that is under scrutiny, and in the process of examining it we witness the first appearance of a suggestion that recurs throughout our investigation. According to this suggestion, Aesthetics and Morality do not, in actual fact, refer to two distinct philosophical spheres but are, rather, 'one and the same'. Reflecting upon this idea, present in both Ancient Greek and twentieth-century Western Philosophy, raises our awareness of how, to be successful, our discussion will have to be led on many levels, ranging from the very abstract (such as the concepts of the good and the beautiful in Plato) to the quite concrete (such as the active influence of moral qualities over aesthetic ones in artworks). Two accounts of aesthetic experience are critically examined but so doing reveals that philosophical definitions in terms of psychology and unique mental events are unlikely to resolve whether, and if so where, the limits of the aesthetic are to be drawn. For that reason we turn to that which aesthetic experience is first and foremost an experience of, namely aesthetic value, in the hope of improving our grasp of the aesthetic in general.

In order to shed light on aesthetic value, and establish whether the contrast with the moral case is more easily drawn in this regard, Chapter 2 addresses the case of art, and the manner in which it can have both aesthetic and moral value. At first, we reflect on a list enumerating the many different reasons why one may value art, and, consequently, consider the various kinds of value that can, often as a direct result of those reasons, be ascribed to art. A distinction is then outlined between two ways in which we can value art – either for its own sake or for some ulterior purpose it may serve. Having thus singled out that value that may properly be called intrinsic, we examine the relation between the kinds of value that tend to add or feed in to this intrinsic value. As we shall see, there are three kinds of value in particular that are relevant in this respect, namely aesthetic, moral, and artistic value. How are we to understand the connections between these three kinds of value, we will ask, assuming that they are indeed distinct from one another?

In Part II, therefore, our principal concern is art; or, to be more precise, our appreciation of it. Even though art is not the only, nor perhaps even the most representative, kind of object of aesthetic appreciation, it nonetheless presents a particularly interesting case in virtue of the moral content it may have. In art, aesthetic and moral character often meet, so to speak, and for that reason it is highly relevant to our enquiry. For, while art certainly can be viewed both from an aesthetic and a moral perspective, the over-riding question is whether these two perspectives can exercise some influence upon one another. More specifically, we will ask, to what extent (if indeed any) does the moral value of an artwork influence its intrinsic value where that value is cast primarily in aesthetic terms? As we shall see, upholding a distinction between aesthetic and artistic value will serve us well here, because it is one thing to say that moral value influences artistic value, and another to say that it influences aesthetic value – moral value could affect artistic value without therefore necessarily affecting its aesthetic value as such.

We must, however, be careful not to get ahead of ourselves here. For although it does seem uncontroversial to say that one of the reasons why we can value art is because of its moral content, and that one of the kinds of value we ascribe to art is moral value, we have not yet established that art can indeed have any substantial moral content or character to speak of. Chapter 3 thus takes us to task on this matter, and asks whether there is room in our conception of art for some perhaps more cognitively laden kind of value? The obvious place to begin answering this question is by posing another, namely whether art can yield understanding and knowledge in the first place. Step by step, then, we examine which kinds of knowledge art can yield, if any, in order to establish whether it is capable of yielding moral understanding more specifically. Fundamentally, the aim of Chapter 3 is thus to secure the claim that we in a sense started off by assuming, namely that there are some objects of aesthetic appreciation that can actually have non-trivial moral content and value.

Chapter 4 presses on with the over-riding concern of Part II, and deals directly with the possibility that an artwork's moral character may affect its overall worth. Should we, it asks, let a work's moral character influence our appreciation and assessment of that work? Crucially, the question is no longer limited to appreciation, be it aesthetic or artistic, but also includes a more cognitive dimension in assessment. What is at stake here, then, is not merely the way in which we experience or undergo a kind of value, but the manner in which we make an appraisal or judgement about that value when ascribed to an artwork. Roughly speaking, the question can be tackled from two opposite approaches, both of which allow significant advantages. However, both accounts are shown to have difficulties in accommodating for problematic cases in which aesthetic and moral value seem to conflict, or at least to be at odds to the naked eye. As long as the emphasis we place on such cases remains open to discussion, the advantages of neither approach outweigh those of the other conclusively.

Immoral art, or art which promotes a morally reprehensible position or world-view, is thus pivotal to the entire debate, and therefore occupies a central role in Chapter 5. For art that, at least at a first glance, seems both beautiful and yet morally questionable is bound to raise the question of whether the beauty of such art can be held *because* of or *in spite* of its morally flawed character. That is to say, the problem we are confronted with is one of whether moral demerits can, in an artistic context, count as aesthetic merits or not. Although we will explore this question from different angles, one in particular stands out. The idea here is, surprisingly perhaps, that a work's value can be enhanced *in virtue* of its immoral character because imaginatively experiencing certain morally flawed responses can actively deepen our understanding and appreciation of a particular artwork and the subject which it treats. Finally, and following on from this idea, we will consider the subject of censorship, or the question of whether, if we admit that immoral art can at least occasionally have some aesthetic or artistic value precisely because of its morally reprehensible character, immoral art can ever rightfully be censored.

Finally, in Part III we turn to examine the relation between Aesthetics and Morality from a more conceptual point of view. That is to say, by focusing on the notions typically at the very core of either discipline – beauty and moral goodness – we will consider the kind of tie that may be said to link these two concepts metaphysically. Clearly, the concern touches not only on conceptual dependence as such but also on the issue of logical priority, because if one of the two concepts can be shown to stem from or ensue from the other, there is a sense in which the assimilation suggested already in Chapter 1 is not only an appropriate philosophical account of the relation under scrutiny here but also one whereby, ultimately, one is philosophically reducible to the other. In the process of investigating this more targeted relation, we soon get a taste, however, of quite how many variations there seem to be on this theme. For the question of how far we ought to go with regards to conceptual dependence takes many closely related yet distinct expressions. Most notably, there are issues about affective disposition, observational skills, education, discernment and sensitivity, and individual character.

Chapter 6 introduces this set of concerns to us, and places the discussion in a distinctively Kantian context. Famously, Kant claims that beauty is the symbol of Morality. He grounds his position on two powerful descriptions of aesthetic judgement's unique character. This character, however, is special in large part due to its privileged relation to Morality in general and goodness in particular. Its exceptional character is thus first and foremost to be understood in terms of the glimpse it allows us to catch of the highest instantiation of our moral status, namely the idea of moral freedom. Approaching the relation between beauty and moral goodness from a similar angle, Friedrich Schiller picks up on Kant's account, and develops a version of that theory which places an emphasis on education. Against the background of an analysis of his contemporary society, which he saw as riven by fragmentation, Schiller argued that the cultivation of aesthetic taste through the experience of art held the key to restoring a sense of moral cohesion to society.

Another way in which the relation between beauty and goodness may be manifested is to be found in the process whereby aesthetic and moral judgements are made. Chapter 7 highlights the many psychological faculties or mental abilities employed in perceiving and judging beauty, and asks whether they mirror their moral counterparts either in constitution or means. For the distinctive perceptiveness, acuity and sensibility – the exercise of which seems required when we engage with aesthetic and moral value – allow for several similarities that, understandably, have led more than one philosopher to believe that aesthetic and moral sensibility are two instances of one and the same intellectual ability. It is perhaps particularly the manner in which both aesthetic and moral sensibility can be cultivated and refined with time that suggests that what we are dealing with here may be nothing other than one skill with both affective and cognitive elements.

Proceeding along that line of thought, Chapter 8 describes and discusses how the similarities between aesthetic and moral sensibility have caused some philosophers to go further still in their reasoning, and hold that having a certain aesthetic or moral sensibility implies being a certain kind of person in so far as having a refined aesthetic sensibility is symptomatic of being a morally good person. In other words, being able to perceive aesthetic qualities and grasp aesthetic character is indicative of being virtuous, for to have a good heart, so to speak, goes hand in hand with being a good aesthetic agent, and having a virtuous character can be said to reveal refined aesthetic skills. Chapter 8 brings to our attention three theories that build on this idea, and then turns to discuss a weaker formulation of the idea which explores the idea of the moral and aesthetic imagination. In particular, the manner in which our imagination helps us weave narratives crucial to the appropriate aesthetic experience of a work of art is assessed in relation to its possible moral application.

III

While firmly grounded in concerns primarily aesthetic and moral, the questions outlined above clearly raise issues that have strong metaphysical and epistemological undercurrents. The enquiry of Part I is first and foremost directed at the possibility of individuating our subject-area and an exploration of the methodological means by which to ensure such an individuation. The boundaries we try to locate in that process are fundamentally metaphysical in character and any implications the outcome of our enquiry will have will be deeply embedded in difficult ontological problems. Similarly, Part II probes the epistemology of how aesthetic, moral and artistic character is both appreciated and evaluated, and the extent to which certain kinds of value may, or may not, be conceived as independent of one another. In attempting to shed light on whether there are philosophically significant boundaries to be drawn between aesthetic, moral and artistic value respectively, epistemological and metaphysical concerns merge to form a challenging set of particularly pressing yet important questions. Lastly, Part III critically discusses the manner in which we perceive aesthetic qualities and make aesthetic judgements. In addition, it addresses the manner whereby aesthetic and moral concepts can be refined and improved upon. Finally, it urges us to reflect upon the concepts that epitomize aesthetic and moral value, namely beauty and goodness, in order to establish whether these notions are necessarily tied to one another at the level of metaphysics.

The questions brought to our attention by examining the philosophical relation between Aesthetics and Morality are as pressing as they are wide-ranging in their application. As we shall see at various occasions throughout this book, the relation under scrutiny is a changing and flexible one – in some respects the two disciplines are very close, but not so in others. Indeed, if there is one overall lesson to be drawn from this study, it is that in many respects the provision of a neat, catch-all theory is unlikely ever to emerge, or at least not in a way that renders the many problems we shall encounter during our journey obsolete. For one of the sources of richness of this area of investigation is precisely the resistance to overly blunt theorizing. By their natures, the spheres of aesthetic and moral experience are open-ended, and characterized by their ability to absorb new aspects of life as it is lived. It is perhaps unsurprisingly, therefore, that this open-ended character should find its way into the Philosophy of the subject.

PART I

THE LIMITS OF THE AESTHETIC

CHAPTER I

DISENTANGLING THE AESTHETIC

TWO SPHERES OF ENQUIRY?

To philosophize about questions in Aesthetics or Morality is first and foremost to reflect upon and scrutinize value. Aesthetic and moral value, perhaps more than any other kinds of value, answer to our sense of what we consider to be of genuine importance in life, the kind of persons we want to become, and what aims we deem truly meaningful. Aesthetic and moral issues are both deeply intertwined with our relations to other persons (past, present and future), not merely in terms of thought, action and reaction, but also in respect of the opportunities we want to enable them to have and the kind of experiences we want to be available to them. One could say that aesthetic and moral value puts our lives in a certain kind of perspective, one that is simultaneously internal to humankind and yet external to our individual selves; a point of view intimately bound up with what it is to be a person, among others and in oneself.

The relation between the investigative realms of Aesthetics and Morality consequently runs both wide and deep. While the variety of common concerns includes a multitude of issues about the meaning of life, beauty, the pursuit of goodness, the meaning of pleasure, how to live well, and many others, it also draws upon questions specific to the level of ontology, epistemology and methodology. That is to say, not only do our aesthetic and moral evaluations inhabit or touch on many of the same areas of our thought and existence, but they bear significant similarity at a structural level at the same time. Among these questions we find queries about the kind of existence that can be ascribed to aesthetic and moral qualities (how, if at all, do such qualities exist in the world?), what kind of sensibilities we exercise in making aesthetic and moral judgements, and how the awareness of aesthetic and moral value may coincide in the perception and assessment of art.

In fact, the overlap of concerns between Aesthetics and Morality can be seen to be so far-reaching that any rigid separation between the two spheres of enquiry may seem unnecessary, misleading even. For, what purpose would it serve, one may wonder, to isolate two areas of philosophical examination that seem to share not only numerous initial concerns but maybe even the means by which we can grasp their very subject-matter? In other words, given that moral and aesthetic value seem so firmly connected, and that the object of enquiry is the notion of value (and our experience of it) in both cases, should we really draw a dividing line between them? Perhaps Ludwig Wittgenstein was right, then, when he proclaimed that 'Ethics and Aesthetics are one and the same' (1961: §6.421)?[1]

There are several ways in which one can agree with Wittgenstein's claim here. On the one hand, one might want to reply that there is a logical priority between the two disciplines, and that what is true of one (i.e. the first, logically speaking) necessarily follows for the other too. In this vein, philosophers such as A. J. Ayer and J. L. Mackie seem to have worked on the assumption that the results obtained from philosophizing about moral matters can more or less directly be applied to parallel aesthetic cases as well.[2] Morality or Ethics is thus considered to be the primary source of enquiry from which results equally relevant and valid to questions about aesthetic value can be derived.

On the other hand, it is possible to hold that the philosophical domains of Aesthetics and Morality ought not to be divided in so far as the notions central to those spheres of enquiry cannot properly be understood in isolation from one another. According to this view, common among ancient Greek philosophers, separate questions can be formulated for each area of investigation even though there is an important sense in which, ultimately, beauty and moral goodness are inseparable at a conceptual level.

Of these two positive ways of approaching Wittgenstein's suggestion, the latter seems the more interesting. For while the first kind of answer certainly provides a very neat account of the philosophical relation between Aesthetics and Moral Philosophy, it fails in at least two respects: first, it overlooks the numerous differences that (despite their many similarities) *do* prevail between the aesthetic and moral case; second, it assumes that the latter has a logical priority over the former without providing any convincing argumentation for that claim other than that we seem to have more stable, or at least less elusive, material to go on in the case of ethics.

The second line of enquiry seems considerably more promising for – although demonstrably more complex, and to contemporary minds at first sight decidedly suspect – it nonetheless allows for a degree of variety and complexity that seems to reflect our intuitions about the relation between Aesthetics and Morality in at least some important respects. Both Plato and Aristotle raise and discuss questions specific to the philosophy of art (including the function of art and the role of the artist), and yet these concerns are not considered in isolation from other areas of philosophical examination, most notably moral and political philosophy.[3] Indeed, the conceptual proximity of aesthetic and moral value in the accounts presented by Plato and Aristotle is mirrored at the level of vocabulary: one of the main terms for 'art' in Ancient Greek, *techne*, is also implicitly linked to the notions both of craft and of practical wisdom; and the term for 'the beautiful', '*to kalon*', directly refers to the idea of doing something well or right, extending to the idea of the good in itself and even to the notion of hospitality. Where the language seems not to permit of any rigid separation, then, the philosophy seems to follow.

For Plato and Aristotle, all art has a moral nature in virtue of affecting the way in which we see and relate to the world. It does so by directing our sympathies and emotions, where such affective states are considered to be a constitutive element of our broader Morality. Of all the artforms, music is held to be the most directly moral, precisely because it is thought to allow for an un-mediated correlation with our emotions. What is more, and as Plato explains in the *Timaeus*, music is held to originate from the same geometric patterns and formulae as the world itself; music thus becomes essential to our moral education because its principal function is to attune us to the world through the proportions and quantities that we hear in, say, musical rhythm and harmony. That is to say, through learning to listen to and appreciate music, we come to understand the world better, and act more in harmony with it. And since the world has its origin in the divine, and goodness its origin in nature, to temper one's actions through listening to music makes one a better person. Indeed, in the *Republic*, Plato even goes so far as to suggest that, 'when modes of music change, the fundamental laws of the State always change with them' (2003: Book IV, §424).

Plato is less famous for his conception of the moral benefits of music and the arts than for the condemnation of artists and their work that occupies a large part of Book X of his *Republic*. As is well known, representational artforms such as painting and poetry are rejected by Plato principally on account of what is conceived as their metaphysical poverty: if the objects of the world are already themselves mere imitations of the ideal and universal Forms of such objects, as Plato would have us believe, then representational artworks are nothing but imitations of imitations, and thus at two removes from true understanding. For example, the chairs we sit on are, for Plato, better or worse imitations of a kind of universal, ideal chair – what Plato calls a 'Form' – and when we have knowledge of what a chair is it is this Form that we have come to know. It is the Forms that constitute truth and the ultimate reality of things. For Plato, then, to look to an artistic imitation of something as a source of knowledge is to move in the wrong metaphysical direction: instead of moving from potentially illusory representation to ultimate reality (knowledge of Form), one moves from representation further in the direction of illusion.

To modern – and possibly less metaphysically rigid understanding – Plato's objection may seem obscure. Nonetheless, he does identify a problem with art that is both interesting and pressing. This concerns the fact that art itself does not seem to have a corresponding Form (or at least not one that is intelligible). That is to say, we do not have, or do not seem to have, any fully determinate idea of what artworks are supposed to be (either in themselves or in virtue of some function), to do, to look like, etc. So, Plato contends, in having no access to the Form of which worldly art is supposed to be an imitation, we thus have no rational way of determining its imitative success; no way, that is to say, of judging its merit, of evaluating it. The problem, then, becomes one of the measures of artistic excellence being grounded in little other than the vanity of artists and vagaries of audience opinion.

It is interesting to note that although primarily metaphysical in its dimensions, this issue is treated explicitly as a moral and political problem by Plato. For he claims that followers of art become morally immature in being forced, by the nature of art, to be dependent upon others for their opinions and evaluations. And

unlike other instances of immaturity, there is no educational palliative to that caused by art, for the simple reason that there does
not seem to be any rational system that can, once mastered, be
used for the purposes of making true judgements about it.

While these and other disadvantages inherent to art seem sufficient grounds for Plato to expel the dramatic poets from his ideal
republic, Aristotle takes a different view on that matter. Dramatic
poetry, and tragedy in particular, Aristotle argues, is able to act for
the good, and thus indirectly lead to the good of its audience and
participants. It is able to act thus not only by engaging with our
moral imagination (for instance in tying it to moral exemplars
drawn from myth and history), but also by playing a purgative role
for emotions such as anger and fear which, if left undisturbed, will
express themselves in a more socially disruptive manner. Tragedy
and by extension other serious forms of representational art are
thus considered good by Aristotle because their purpose is ultimately defined in terms of the peace and well-being of a properly
functioning society.

For Plato and Aristotle, then, it would be inconceivable to
discuss art independently of its moral and political implications:
one can even say that the very question under scrutiny here would
not even have occurred to them.[4] It hardly needs to be pointed
out, however, that the manner in which art, beauty and aesthetic
value is conceived nowadays has changed considerably, and particularly rapidly in the last hundred years or so. Philosophers of the
twentieth and twenty-first centuries more often than not address
the questions highlighted by Plato and Aristotle about painting,
poetry and tragedy without the wider context of a moral
framework.

There is, then, the simple possibility that we should flatly deny
Wittgenstein's claim. For if, as seems to be the case in our own
day, art is valued for its own sake alone and aesthetic value is
understood purely in terms of sensory and/or intellectual
pleasure, then art would seem to be entirely amoral. To support
this view further, several important differences do seem to
prevail between the aesthetic case and the moral one, not least
with regard to the possible outcome of moral deliberation and
the contrasting lack thereof from most aesthetic contemplation.
Philosophizing about moral matters tends to have implications in
respect of certain kinds of action or behaviour, whereas reflecting

on aesthetic perception and experience at best only leads to such practical consequences indirectly. We may, for example, wish to learn to paint in a certain way or acquire a certain sculpture as a result of contemplating some thing aesthetically, but this cannot be said to be the *aim* of thinking philosophically about art.

It might also be said that to adopt a philosophical strategy whereby the differences between the aesthetic and moral cases are emphasized can yield some significant advantages over the alternative approach by which these divergences are conceded yet not deemed decisive. For one, it invites us to adhere to a model in which relative simplicity governs: if the aesthetic and moral spheres of enquiry are entirely detached from one another, and philosophers working on aesthetic matters can operate in an environment that is more or less hermetically sealed off from the moral realm, several of the most difficult questions in Aesthetics – such as those of the possible censorship of artworks on moral grounds – do not even arise. And what more efficient way to rebuke a philosophical problem, one may wonder, than by denying that there is a difficulty to address in the first place?

Perhaps, then, what one's response to Wittgenstein's suggestion depends upon is first and foremost the level of intricacy with which one understands the relation between the aesthetic and the moral spheres, and the philosophical importance one is willing to accord any such relations. No one doubts that representational artforms, such as painting, tragedy or novels, can have specifically moral content; but there is much disagreement about how such content might bear a relationship to an artwork's aesthetic or artistic character, or whether any putative moral consequences issuing from the viewing of a painting, or the reading of a novel, are in any way germane to our experience of such things as artworks. Interestingly, and as we shall soon see, any accurate account of the relation is likely to be subject to continuous change not only in so far as cases that appear to be similar may in fact call for radically different accounts, but also to the extent that the aesthetic and the moral may demonstrate close interrelation in some respects, and yet call for a fairly rigid separation in others.

As our principal concern here is with the implications this intricate relation holds for the discipline of Aesthetics, our investigation will first be required to delve into the notion seemingly at its very heart, namely aesthetic experience. For any attempt to account for the relation between aesthetic value and moral value will have to be based on a good understanding of that which is most distinctively aesthetic. In other words, if Aesthetics and Ethics are to be 'one and the same' in any philosophically significant sense, we will first need an understanding of aesthetic experience from which we can establish what, if anything, extends into the moral dimension.

WHAT MAKES AN EXPERIENCE AESTHETIC?

Underlying the question of what makes an experience aesthetic is the assumption that it is possible to give one unified theory of aesthetic experience. This assumption, though reasonable in some ways, may nonetheless prove unfounded, for part of the aim in trying to define aesthetic experience is precisely to establish whether there can be such a thing as *the* aesthetic experience; and if so, whether it can be accounted for in general terms. One source of concern in this regard may be the great variety of kinds of things that can be objects of aesthetic appreciation: not only things but also persons, events and aspects of the natural world can be appreciated for their aesthetic character.

In addition, there is considerable diversity among both artforms and artworks (even within the same artform) that populate the museums, concert halls and galleries that we visit on a regular basis. Another, perhaps more understated, reason for scepticism here may be the multitude of ways in which one can engage with artworks or objects of aesthetic appreciation: to engage aesthetically with some thing we must not only exercise our various senses (and combinations thereof), but we may also need to set in motion different elements of our aesthetic phenomenology, such as aesthetic emotion, judgement and pleasure, to name the most obvious ones. Clearly, this heterogeneity is a good starting-point for those who want to deny the possibility of there being *one* aesthetic experience and one corresponding definition of it.

More optimistically, however, several interesting theories have been put forward in the last 50 years or so in an attempt to pinpoint what it is that individuates a distinctively aesthetic state of mind. In particular, two psychological accounts of aesthetic experience have been widely discussed, and it is interesting to note that neither focuses on any particular element of our phenomenology in isolation from the others. Rather than isolating one component of aesthetic experience, such as aesthetic pleasure for example, and developing the importance of that component's role in aesthetic experience, aesthetic experience is first and foremost discussed as a kind of mental state in its own right.

According to the first of these two accounts, an aesthetic experience is a mental state characterized by three features, namely unity, complexity and intensity. In the words of one of the theory's chief proponents, Monroe Beardsley,

> [a] person is having an aesthetic experience during a particular stretch of time if and only if the greater part of his mental activity during that time is united and made pleasurable by being tied to the form and qualities of a sensuously presented or imaginatively intended object on which his primary attention is concentrated. (1969: 5)

An object of aesthetic appreciation is valuable in so far as it is capable of yielding experiences of this sort and, furthermore, an artwork is to be understood as the kind of thing that aims to give us such experiences.

Beardsley's theory, although perhaps a little simplistic at first sight, has the advantage of highlighting features that are not only very familiar to us from aesthetic experience, but which are also quite easy to identify. In addition, it draws a distinction between aesthetic experience and a more wide-ranging kind of aesthetic engagement in a way that alleviates some of the philosophical pressure placed on the former notion. For Beardsley, only a very limited account of our 'aesthetic life' can be explained in terms of aesthetic experience, and so, he holds, the theory cannot actually be undermined by the claim that not all aspects of our 'aesthetic life' are characterized by unity, complexity and intensity.

The point is indeed a crucial one to address, for famously, George Dickie has held that Beardsley's suggestion cannot be said to define aesthetic experience successfully since there is no principled reason to suppose that our aesthetic experiences must always be unified, intense and complex. In fact, Dickie continues, aesthetic experience does not seem to need to have any of those features. Moreover, it is pointed out that the three features are not dependent on one another in so far as an experience can be complex and intense, say, without being unified. For example, our aesthetic experiences of Morandi's still-life paintings need not be either unified, complex or intense, nor would they have to be, say, intense if they were complex and unified.

Beardsley's manoeuvre thus aims to undermine objections such as these by limiting what can rightly be called aesthetic experience to a small and select group of mental events. Unfortunately, this shift fails ultimately to save his account: addressing concerns about a particular theory's restrictions simply by narrowing down the remit of that to which the theory is intended to apply is rarely a particularly successful philosophical method, and is certainly not so in the present case. For unless one is willing to concede that the notion of aesthetic experience should only be applicable, as Beardsley specifies, on special occasions, the claim that aesthetic experience is to be defined in terms of unity, intensity and complexity is just not credible. However, a closer inspection reveals that this conjecture stands on ground no more solid than the original claim, for there simply seems to be no principled reason why aesthetic experience could not be more widely (and frequently) applied – unless, that is, one builds those constraints into its very definition as Beardsley does.

A second attempt at defining aesthetic experience in psychological terms claims that when we engage in aesthetic contemplation, we adopt a unique mental stance mainly characterized by a certain kind of detachment. For when we appreciate things aesthetically, we do not look at the object for any practical function it may serve. Instead, we assess an object solely for its aesthetic character. This 'aesthetic attitude' is based on a kind of attention that is contemplative, discerning, and not directed at anything beyond the object.

In this vein, Jerome Stolnitz has argued that when we have aesthetic experiences, our sensory capacities, unconstrained by practical concerns, simply appreciate the perceivable form of things. In contradistinction to our usual perceptual operations, which might involve assessments of a given object in relation to its function or its value in relation to, say, our survival or social status, the aesthetic attitude is marked by a detached and open awareness. In Stolnitz's words, the aesthetic attitude is a 'disinterested and sympathetic attention to any object of awareness whatever for its own sake alone' (1960: 34). Importantly, this non-instrumental way of contemplating things seems to capture something fundamental to aesthetic experience and, moreover, renders intelligible the considerable mental participation of the perceiver. By placing the *locus* of the aesthetic in the very foundations of the subject's attitude, it becomes possible to explain the way in which any kind of object can be viewed aesthetically, be it a church, a seascape, or a person.

For all their advantages, however, aesthetic attitude theories nonetheless tend to rest on the assumption that for each and every time we take a purely aesthetic interest in the object of appreciation, we do so not only in a unique fashion, but also in a manner identical across cases of aesthetic appreciation. In the first instance, it is not actually entirely clear that all aesthetic experiences can be characterized by this kind of uniformity. Considering, for example, that the experience of looking at a painting or reading a poem is bound to comprise a great number of different mental states, and a great variety among them. More importantly, though, one may wonder how the aesthetic attitude can be said to define the aesthetic as such when it cannot itself be accounted for independently of that very same notion? If, in other words, a large part of the *raison d'être* of the notion of an aesthetic attitude is precisely to demarcate that which is distinctively *aesthetic*, and that attitude is itself cashed out as an attitude focused on taking an *aesthetic* interest in an object, then the very idea of the aesthetic is presupposed by it. There is, then, a circularity here that seems to preclude the possibility of the aesthetic attitude making any serious philosophical progress with regard to defining aesthetic experience.

In fact, difficulties such as these have led some philosophers to argue that the notion of aesthetic attitude is a philosophical ghost, unjustifiably sneaked into our analysis of aesthetic experience.[5] In reality, it is held, there is nothing more at play here than simple attention, as the disinterestedness concerns only the *motivation* and not the *nature* of the contemplation in question. In this spirit, John Hospers claims that the aesthetic attitude is 'at least, a welter of overlapping ideas, and at worst, a phantom no longer worth chasing' (1982: 353).

What does seem certain, however, is that the aesthetic interest we take in things, persons and situations differs according to context. Sometimes our aesthetic experience is reflective or contemplative, and at other times we indulge in a more sensory kind of involvement. Sometimes the experience is a passive one, such as when a piece of music seems to sweep us off our feet. At other times it seems more active, such as when we are trying to piece together a complex poem. At other times again, things appear to make sense of us and at others they call for us to make sense of them. Obviously, these differences are to be explained not only in terms of the kinds of things that we are appreciating (say Wagner's operas on the one hand and Le Corbusier's architectural constructions on the other), but may also vary in accordance with our general mood or focus. Aesthetic experiences are particularly rich and diverse mental events, and this presents a philosophical challenge that any aesthetic attitude theorist will find difficult to overcome. For even if such a theorist concedes that there can be *several* aesthetic attitudes, she will still have to bring those various attitudes together under one 'umbrella concept' eventually, if only to explain why they may be thought of as instances of the same kind of mental event in the first place. Similarly, it will cause serious concern to any defender of Beardsley's theory since it is at best very difficult to both characterize all aesthetic experience in any of the terms prescribed by his account and admit that those terms are dependent on one another in the manner specified.

All in all, perhaps the most that can be said in definitional terms about aesthetic experience, then, is that it involves some or all (depending on the particular circumstances) of the following kinds of mental states: pleasurable appreciation of form and design, detachment from practical concerns, discernment of aesthetically salient or resonant features, perception of aesthetic qualities such as elegance and balance, attention to the ways in which the formal, aesthetic and expressive qualities have been manufactured in the case of artworks, awareness of any such projected properties in the case of nature, contemplation of ambiguity, awareness of an object's emotional or representational content.[6] Probably, were we to analyse the kinds of awareness or perception that can participate in what we call aesthetic experience, we would end up with a list that was very long indeed. If only for that reason, it is doubtful that the key to a successful conceptual analysis of aesthetic experience could lie in attempting to outline necessary and sufficient conditions for a specific mental state to qualify as distinctively aesthetic. Rather, it may be found in a whole set of psychological states that are combined differently from case to case.

In this, then, we appear to end exactly where we started. Fundamentally, it seems that aesthetic experience is best characterized in terms of the experience of aesthetic value, and since aesthetic value can take a multitude of different shapes and forms, so can our experience of it. But the exploration has certainly not been a meaningless one, since one of the most important features of aesthetic experience lies precisely in the fact that it cannot easily be delimited and neatly cut off from all its non-aesthetic counterparts. All that has been shown so far, then, is that a definition of aesthetic experience in terms of necessary and sufficient conditions along the lines suggested above seems unlikely to succeed.

Of course, this is not to say that there can be no such thing as aesthetic experience *tout court*, or that the notion is empty. Rather, and on a more positive note, it does seem to suggest that the aesthetic, in virtue of having a deeply fluent and non-restrictive character, may be particularly open to influences from neighbouring areas. The question that confronts us, therefore, has less to do with pinpointing the conditions in which an experience or object should be characterized in distinctively and uncontroversially aesthetic terms, than it does with exploring the limits of the term's application. How far does aesthetic experience and value go? In which cases does it impinge directly on other areas of our experience and thought, and in which cases do other areas of our experience and thought impinge directly on it?

WHAT ARE THE BOUNDARIES OF THE AESTHETIC?

If our preliminary investigation suggests that the notion of aesthetic experience is, at least in the first instance, best understood as involving several kinds of perceptual states with a focus on aesthetic value, then in one sense our achievement in the previous section has merely been to push our initial concern away from the idea of a single and unique mental attitude, and back onto that of aesthetic value. Thus the questions we began by outlining may now take on a revised guise. On the one hand, we may ask 'How exactly are we to conceive of the relation between aesthetic and moral value in objects of aesthetic appreciation?' On the other hand, we may pose the question 'What does the sensibility exercised in aesthetic perception, emotion, judgement and discernment have in common (if anything) with moral sensibility?'

The second of these concerns will be addressed in Part III, where sensibility to value will be our principal subject. The epistemology of aesthetic experience(s) affords both similarities and dissimilarities with the moral case, and perhaps even more interestingly, may be said to share some overriding aims with its moral counterpart. We may take the example of Plato, for whom aesthetic judgements are inseparable from their moral application, and where the notion of beauty is clearly understood in terms of motivating us towards truth and goodness, to suggest the scale and import of what is at stake in the raising of such issues. For what is being asked here are questions that occupy the very heart of our notion of humanity.

The first set of questions – about the relation between moral and aesthetic value in any given object of aesthetic appreciation – will be the subject of Part II, where we will examine the way in which aesthetic value may be influenced by moral value in the context of artistic appreciation. For it is one thing to infer that the ancient Greek experience of art was conceived squarely in moral terms, but quite another to extend this expectation into our own age, when suggestions that artworks may have moral ends, or may require moral interpretations, are more often than not greeted with surprise. Indeed, as we shall see, simply raising philosophical questions may lead to a clearer grasp of the notion of aesthetic value and how, and when, it is to be distinguished from other kinds of value.

Delimiting the boundaries of the aesthetic as a sphere of enquiry is thus not so much a given starting-point for philosophical investigation into the realm of Aesthetics as a critical examination in itself. As we have already seen, an exploration into the notion of aesthetic experience seeking to isolate a definition in stringent terms seems unlikely to succeed. This is not to say, however, that a conceptual analysis or elucidation of both the ontological and epistemological characteristics of aesthetic value may not, at the very least, lead us to a greater understanding of how aesthetic value exists and acts in the world through our experience of it. What we must do, then, is press on with questions such as 'Are there any limits to the applicability of aesthetic value?' and 'How, if at all, is aesthetic experience to be cordoned off from the rest of our experience?' in the hope of gaining some of the clarification we need in order to pinpoint with greater specification where the aesthetic ends and other spheres begin.

These questions, which lie at the heart of Philosophical Aesthetics, are not easily answered. This book is concerned primarily with exploring the shared territory of moral and aesthetic value, and this boundary of the aesthetic domain will be at the centre of what we hope to uncover. It is perhaps worth remembering, however, that although our inclinations when considering the aesthetic are to consider it as a special, restricted sphere, brought into play only in the rarefied atmosphere of the art gallery or concert hall, this is not necessarily the most fruitful way to proceed. As we saw in the Introduction, and as we shall see further when we consider accounts such as those of Immanuel Kant in the third part of this book, the boundaries of the aesthetic actually lie at a much greater conceptual distance than when considered more neatly as the Philosophy of fine art. And, in particular, the question of where the aesthetic ends and the moral begins gains in prominence.

It is important to note that the boundaries of the aesthetic may require to be cast slightly differently according to context. In a very influential article on this topic, Ronald Hepburn (1966) argues that several significant philosophical distinctions prevail between the aesthetic experience of art and that of nature. Among them is the fact that since human beings are both *in* and *part of* nature, we are typically involved with nature both in the capacity of actors and spectators. Unlike an artwork, a real landscape, say, does not lead or direct its perceivers' aesthetic responses, at least not in quite the same way. Natural objects of aesthetic appreciation, Hepburn explains, are not set apart from their environment; they are in this sense 'frameless'.

Admitting this distinction, the question of which of the two kinds of aesthetic experience should take logical or conceptual priority immediately arises. On the one hand, one might hold that the experience of nature should be understood in terms of our experience of art; that we only begin to consider nature as an object of aesthetic appreciation once we have learnt how to observe, appreciate and enjoy works of art.[7] For example, it is possible that in order to appreciate the aesthetic character of a mountainous landscape, as opposed to perceiving its blocking of our path, we require a former encounter with an artwork that would enable us to 'notice' that, all along, as it were, the mountains are beautiful. On the other hand, one might equally argue that our appreciation of the said artwork was only made possible by our already having encountered such experiences in the natural world. On one such view, the perceiver of such natural beauty is an active participant in the sense that she is perceptually immersed in the natural world, suggesting perhaps that this kind of engagement should be the model for our aesthetic appreciation of art.[8]

Clearly, our conception of aesthetic experience – and thereby aesthetic value – will depend on the kind of case one considers paradigmatic of aesthetic appreciation, and if only for that reason, it is interesting to reflect upon the question raised by Hepburn and discussed at length in the area of Aesthetics now best known as 'Environmental Aesthetics'. Nevertheless, it is important to bear in mind that rather than there being one definitive form that aesthetic experience is supposed to take, there may, instead, be a wide-ranging set of instances which, while enormously varied in terms of their perceptual content, all share some crucial feature in virtue of which they are properly deemed aesthetic. Aesthetic value is the value that a thing, person or event has in virtue of its distinctively aesthetic qualities. But a good deal more will have to be said about those qualities and the way in which they are influenced by other kinds of qualities if the notion of a kind of specifically aesthetic experience is to be imbued with substantial philosophical content.

PRELIMINARY CONCLUSIONS: LOCATING THE AESTHETIC

We have so far raised many more questions than we have even tried to answer with regard to the notion of the aesthetic: we have broached concerns to do with aesthetic experience, value, appreciation and assessment, and we have listed or hinted at a panoply of queries for each. Nonetheless, coming to see how both wide-ranging and profound this set of questions is has revealed several interesting aspects of the aesthetic that we will have to contend with from now on.

Perhaps particularly prominently, we have seen that instead of proceeding along a relatively traditional rhetorical structure whereby one begins by demarcating that which is distinctively aesthetic in view of disentangling it from its neighbouring spheres of influence, it will in this case prove more fruitful to reverse that order of investigation. That is to say, in order to succeed in getting a better grasp of the notion in question, we will first have to extricate it from other areas of examination. Proper conceptual analysis of aesthetic experience and value will thus have to be preceded by an exploration of those notions' relations to adjoining philosophical disciplines. It is, in other words, in contrasts and comparisons that the beginning of a satisfactory answer into the question of what the aesthetic really is will most probably be found.

In this sense, then, exploring the relation between Aesthetics and Morality is more of a preparation or groundwork than a consequence or ramification for any thorough philosophical examination of the notion of the aesthetic. For, in virtue of their joint focus on value, and the shared goals and aspirations outlined at the very opening of this chapter, the most obvious and perhaps even threatening neighbouring discipline that may serve this comparative role is Morality or Ethics. Threatening, because if Wittgenstein and his followers are to be believed, then Aesthetics and Ethics are to be amalgamated, and history has shown that such a merger is rarely to the advantage of Aesthetics, at least in terms of philosophical discourse. If, however, it can be established that aesthetic value is an entirely legitimate kind of value alongside moral value, and that there is therefore no risk for the former to be completely reduced to the latter, we can proceed with the more epistemological side of our enquiry. For Aesthetics and Morality may be both practically and conceptually close without being 'one and the same'; they may overlap in some significant respects without ceasing to have their own distinctive character.

CHAPTER 2

THE VALUES OF ART

WHY WE VALUE ART

Whether we are enthusiasts or sceptics about art, connoisseurs or amateurs, it seems impossible to deny that art makes a profound difference to our life and culture. If there were no such thing as art in the world, our daily interactions with both persons, past and future events, and our environments would be unrecognizable in several important respects. For one thing, there would be no sense in which we could study history or the evolution of ideas through artistic movements or theories. Architecture, for example, would most probably be reduced to the mere production of buildings, and fail to express a certain period's ideals, aspirations and values. Similarly, we would have no means beyond records and documentation with which to capture the spirit of significant political and social events. We would, in other words, have to do without works such as Picasso's *Guernica*, which manages to portray and eternalize the horror and injustice of the Spanish Civil War in the most human of terms on a single canvas. Without art, moreover, we would lack those sources of interpretation and elucidation to which we can return time and time again in order to shed light on our own experiences and thought-processes. That is to say, we could not engage repeatedly with fictional works such as Shakespeare's *Macbeth* or Jean-Luc Godard's *Contempt*, for example, in an attempt to gain a better understanding of our own life, or of a specific situation we find ourselves in. The characters we encounter in literature – and on stage, screen and canvas, in marble, bronze and even musical sound – expand the range and variety of our acquaintance enormously, and often help us to see things from a certain angle, or to decide on a particular course of action. Last but not least, a world without art would be unrecognizable in virtue of its lacking one of our main sources of pleasure and delight. The enjoyment afforded by our involvement with a favourite art gallery, or even just a single painting, that we can come back to again and again, or the consolation offered by a much loved work of music; without such adornments to our existence, our life would be both less rich and, arguably, less distinctively human.

Art thus adds a dimension to our life that enables us to relate to persons, places and events in the manner in which we do. This is not to say, of course, that there is only *one* way in which art invites us to connect with the world around us. For art varies so widely both in form and content that it would be nothing short of misleading to suggest that it encourages us to view our surrounding circumstances in one way only. Instead, the avenues that art invites us to explore – and so the respects in which it affects our life – are infinite both in style and substance, and originality and novelty in this regard is and has perhaps always been one of the main aims of art.

It is important to note from the outset that the diversity that pertains to art and its appreciation operates on at least two distinct levels. First, there is considerable variety with regard to the means with which we appreciate works belonging to different artforms and artistic genres. Clearly, the manner in which we engage with a sonata by Mozart, say, will differ significantly from the way in which we appreciate a sculpture by Henry Moore. Similarly, our attitude to a strongly historical and political painting, such as David's *Napoleon*, will differ markedly from the way in which we are likely to approach an abstract work by Mark Rothko.

Second, great divergences occur across individual experiences of art. After all, my experience of Moore's *Reclining Figures* at Kenwood House in London, for example, may differ quite substantially not only from your appreciation of it, but even from my own past (or indeed future) experience of that particular work. My appreciation, for example, might initially have focused on its figurative clarity, on its representational qualities, whereas now it might be more concerned with the sense in which each figure seems to present the abstract of incompleteness, relying on the combination to suggest wholeness. Nothing is fixed, in other words, when it comes to our appreciation of art: be it on the level of form and material, function and design, intention and experience, or simply one person and the next, or even the same person at different times: our relations with artworks as both creators and consumers remain open.

As soon as we begin to reflect on all this diversity, a set of pressing questions centred around the heterogeneity of art arises.[1]

Could it be the case that art and its appreciation is too varied a category to be accounted for in general terms? Will it, in other words, really be possible to provide a unitary answer to the question of why we value art? Is it even necessary to do so?

The challenge set here is a difficult one to fend off as there are very convincing reasons to answer the two questions mentioned directly above negatively. For it takes no more than a quick glance to see that, in reality, we value art for all sorts of different reasons. From the ecclesiastical art of medieval Europe to the Conceptual Art of 1970s New York, what we today think of as art has performed a manifold of roles, many of which have little in common. Much of the traditional art and craft of Native American cultures, for example, allows for few points of comparison with Monet's paintings of water-lilies.

Furthermore, the reasons for valuing art differ not only across different eras, but also from one culture to another. In certain closed societies, rather like the totalitarian cultures of Soviet Russia or Maoist China, art is valued mainly for the socio-political purpose it may serve, such as promoting a utopian world-view or reinforcing political myths. In contrast, in democratic countries, it has been precisely art's apolitical possibilities that have been fore-grounded and emphasized. And all, of course, with numerous exceptions in every case.

In addition, and as already mentioned, reasons for valuing art may vary considerably from one person to another: some of us engage with art mainly because of the relaxation and pleasure it may afford, whereas others appreciate art first and foremost for the way in which it may yield insights into certain characters or sit-uations, or educate us about certain kinds of events. It may do so, for example, by representing things we don't know much about, or presenting a certain perspective on things we do know about from a new angle.[2]

Objections to the idea that there could be one underlying reason for why we value art have frequently been levelled. Malcolm Budd, in his *Values of Art*, has explained that there is in fact not just one but two main worries about the allegedly unitary value of art. The first objection states that:

> it is necessary to give an irreducibly disjunctive account of value across the arts, because for each art form – music,

painting, sculpture, architecture, literature, dance – there is a distinct kind of value: the value of a work of art of a particular art form *as* of that form is different for each art form. According to this version of the objection, there is the value of music as music, the value of painting as painting, the value of sculpture as sculpture, and so on, and there is no overarching value that unifies this set of values, which form a heterogeneous collection. (1995: 2)

So, according to Budd's first objection, it seems overly ambitious to postulate a unified theory of the value of art on the simple grounds that the different nature of each form of art implies a system of value that is internal to the conditions of that art being itself. But if that does not seem to present a grave enough challenge, the objection follows the divisions within art, finding that each sub-division of each artform itself has its own distinct and irreducible nature, and seems thus to require its own system of value. This second objection:

presses the point further by claiming that it is necessary to give an irreducibly disjunctive account of value within each art, since each art form admits works of art of different natures and aims and these various kinds of work have values specific to them. So within the art of music, there is the value of a song as a song, the value of a symphony as a symphony, and so on for the other musical genres; and within each of the other arts, there is a distinct kind of value for each artistic genre that falls within that art. (1995: 2)

As Budd suggests, the objection indicates something of a *reductio ad absurdum* of the attempt to provide a unitary account of art's value, since it is possible to find features that not only mark a song out as a song, and thus suggest it be valued on that basis, but also the features that mark out a folk song from a *lied* or a Bruckner symphony from one by Brahms until, eventually, you find yourself operating with a different scale of value for each individual movement of each of the four symphonies by Brahms. And if each artistic object requires its own particular kind of value, the idea of value becomes at best unhelpful and at worst unusable.[3]

So what, if anything, saves us from this infinite regress of the value of art? Is there any sense in which it will be possible to speak of a unified theory of artistic value? To find out, we must begin by thinking about these questions in terms of our experience. For it is, after all, the experience that we have or stand to gain from art that is valuable in the first instance. That is to say, art is valuable to us first and foremost because of the experience we have of it, and it is that experience which can, in turn, be valued for different reasons. Indeed, as we shall see throughout this book, it is the ingredient of individual experience that seems to hold the key to the best understanding of many of the most central features of aesthetic and moral value and the interactions between them. We shall therefore return to this question further along our journey. For now, however, it will be wise to get a better grasp of the range of kinds of value art may have by exploring some of the things we tend to have in mind when we think of art's value in general.

KINDS OF VALUE

We now know that the task ahead of us is not only made difficult by the fact that the reasons for which we value art vary enormously, but is also further complicated by the idea that we must at least attempt to unify this multiplicity with the possibility of an underlying value for art in general. Since we have seen that art can be understood in terms as diverse as those of cultivation and civilization, education, questioning and self-expression, let us turn to characterize in more detail the range of experiences that art can yield. So doing will bring us closer to an understanding of the ways in which our experience of art reveals a more or less tightly knit set of values, all of which may contribute to or participate in the overall value of art and our appreciation of it.

At first glance, art seems capable of having at least the following kinds of value: cognitive, social, educational, historical, sentimental, religious, economic, therapeutic, moral, political, and purely aesthetic value.[4] One may say that an artwork can have as many different kinds of value as there are perspectives from which that work can be evaluated. Clearly, it won't always be easy to demarcate these kinds of value from one another, or indeed to establish with certainty which of them dominates in a particular artwork. Nonetheless, it is possible to make some progress and attain some clarification on the matter by briefly surveying the principal kinds of experience and, by extension, value, that objects of artistic appreciation may afford.

Although we know very little about the circumstances in which the cave paintings at Lascaux in France or the rock carvings at Tanum in Western Sweden were produced or experienced, it seems fairly uncontroversial to hold that one of the main ways in which their value may best be understood is in terms of the expression they gave to a social or community identity.[5] Cave paintings and rock carvings can thus be seen to have acted as a unifying factor for a group and express some kind of binding identity for its members. Indeed, it is most probably in terms of their *social value*, or function as a point of focus for the early human communities, that they would have primarily been valuable. Obviously, this kind of value can be found in artworks of all ages. The social value of dance and theatre, for example, is often witnessed whether it be very old tribal dances or entirely contemporary ballet. Notably, too, when contemporary government arts agencies, such as the Arts Councils in Great Britain, are assessing projects as to their meriting financial support, the value such prospective art projects would have at a social and community level are among the most prominent of the considerations nowadays brought to bear on the assessment.

In addition to the social value that cave art had for its contemporaries, these objects of artistic appreciation clearly nowadays also have an *archaeological* or *historical value*. For, to us, they stand as testimonies to cultures and peoples past; they not only corroborate some of the things we already know about them but also hint at new avenues of research and exploration into our joint history. By acquainting ourselves with them, we get a better grasp of some aspects of our predecessors' lives and belief systems. Cave paintings may, along with some other archaeological artefacts, therefore be considered to bridge a gulf between the 'here and now' and things long gone.

Art can also have *religious value*. The plainchant that many of us now admire for its serene and peaceful qualities was, in fact, developed from Christian liturgical practices as one of the principal forms of worship. Similarly, the stained glass and sculptures that we now see adorning the architectural masterpieces of Chartres Cathedral and York Minster were originally esteemed and cherished primarily for their religious value. Features such as the exceptional height of the interiors, the multitude of vertical lines, and pointed arches, were all conceived as leading first the eye, and then the mind, toward the contemplation of heaven, while the glass and sculpture, in addition to adding to the splendour and mystery that these buildings must have represented to their early visitors, told and retold stories from the Bible.

In this sense, too, art such as the aforementioned stained glass and sculpture can be said to have *cognitive value*: a clear part of its role is, or at least was initially, to represent scenes and convey narratives from Christianity's foundational myths. As such, stained-glass windows and sculptures in churches and cathedrals had a clearly defined *educational* role. Interestingly, it is not only art that sets out to represent features of the world that may have cognitive value in this manner. Art that centres on the representation and exploration of concepts may also be understood primarily in terms of its conceptual value. Joseph Kosuth's *One and Three Chairs*, for example, prompts us to grapple with the metaphysical (and distinctively Platonic) question of which is the more real – the definition (the 'Form' or 'Idea' to use Plato's terminology) of the chair, the representation of the chair, or the actual chair. In a similar vein, Michael Craig-Martin's *An Oak Tree*, which presents us with a glass of water on a glass shelf and a label explaining that what you see is in actual fact an oak tree, forces us to engage with issues of conventional nomenclature and the neo-Aristotelian doctrine of transubstantiation. What all these cases have in common, despite the many ways in which they differ from one another, then, is that beyond the purely sensory, emotional or imaginative aspects of the artistic experience, the contemplation of such artworks yields knowledge of some kind.

More common, and as we have already touched upon, is for artworks to convey knowledge that has more of a historical rather than a purely philosophical focus. To our minds, Jacques Louis David's paintings such as *The Death of Marat*, for example, represent scenes from French *socio-political history*. Having said that, at the time of their inception, they served to monumentalize the origins and flowering of France's new republic and empire. Similarly, Velazquez's depictions of the court of Philip IV of Spain, such as portrayed in *Las Meninas* for example, are valuable in giving us a sense of the splendour of that court, the extravagance of its entertainments, as well as Philip's more private interests in hunting and falconry. Again, at the time, such depictions may have served to bolster recent memory, and to feed more generally into the power and majesty of the Spanish throne. Indeed, many of the paintings that we now consider as timeless were initially conceived and commissioned with a view to economic and political implications such as these. One of the principal motivations behind the artistic flowering that surrounded the court of the Medicis in Florence is best understood in terms of political self-promotion and economic consolidation, regardless of the fact that the artists themselves may have understood their work's value primarily in terms of the science of pictorial representation or, in the case of sacred paintings, of its religious function as an act of, and aid to, worship.

By contrast, in the eighteenth century, the conception applied particularly to the literary arts was widely realigned to emphasize the *sentimental* or *affective value* of a work. The stirring of a reader's emotions came to be considered not just as a means to an end, as in the case, say, of religious art, but as an end in itself, valuable in enriching the private, emotional lives of the reader. Additionally, too, as the understanding of morality shifted from an exclusively rational one, to one that took into account the feelings of moral agents, such sentimental works also came to be conceived in terms of moral education. Novels such as Richardson's *Clarissa*, or Rousseau's *Julie*, for example, were designed to engage and exercise the sympathies of their readers and align them emotionally with moral codes rooted in sentiment.

Indeed, from Rousseau to Dostoevsky, this sense in which art and literature act on our moral psychology has been one of the principal ways in which the putative *moral value* of art has been construed. Yet, and as we saw in our discussion of Plato in Chapter 1, art's potential for moral value has been understood in many different ways, from simply exercising our sense of moral outrage and horror – such as in the case of The Art Workers' Coalition's *Question: And babies? Answer: And babies*, the main constituent of which is a photograph of several dead Vietnamese women and children piled up on a dirt road in My Lai in 1969 – to attempting to realign our traditional moral sympathies – such as in the opera *Carmen*, where Bizet disrupts his audience's habitual inclination to side with the noble Don José and leads them to sympathize with the socially and morally transgressive Carmen.

Finally for our purposes, there is the question of art's purely *aesthetic value*. Certainly for the last 100 years or so, a good deal of art may be said to have been conceived largely in terms of its having aesthetic value, or of its yielding primarily aesthetic experiences.[6] Nowadays, it is fair to say that we tend to think of aesthetic value, or at least beauty and aesthetic pleasure, as the paradigmatic kind of value that art can afford, and the reward it can bring a good part of why we seek to engage with art in the first place. What is more, much of the art that was originally intended to be valued in one of the ways described above (e.g. political or social) is now valued first and foremost in virtue of the distinctively aesthetic experience it can yield. Art and aesthetic value, or the artistic and the aesthetic, are thus often assumed to go hand in hand. If so, the concern we started off by raising – to do with whether there can be such a thing as *the* value of art – may become a question for the philosophy of aesthetic experience: if the value of art is at least principally to be cashed out in terms of its aesthetic worth, then the unitary account one might be searching for may perhaps be found in aesthetic value itself.

As a preliminary conclusion, then, we may put forward the following: aesthetic value seems particularly crucial to the appreciation and worth of art. The question therefore arises of how, if indeed at all, we are to distinguish aesthetic value and artistic value from one another. The issue is pressing in so far as it may be central to our understanding of what the expression 'artistic value' really refers to. Before addressing this aspect of our investigation directly, however, let us turn to a distinction that divides all the kinds of value that one may be inclined to ascribe to art into two distinct groups.

INTRINSIC VALUE AND EXTRINSIC VALUE

The distinction between intrinsic and extrinsic value is particularly pertinent to an examination of art's value in so far as it concerns such value's primary source, and the question of whether that source is internal or external to art itself. Thus we speak of *intrinsic value*, on the one hand, as the kind of value that some thing may have merely for its own sake; the kind of value some thing has in virtue of what it is independently of anything else. On the other hand, *extrinsic value* is the kind of value that some thing has because of its relation to some other thing. Extrinsic value is here to be distinguished in part from instrumental value, which is a form of extrinsic value, and which concerns the *way* in which we value something in respect of its function in leading to some end or other.[7]

What, then, are we to say of art? Is the value of art intrinsic or extrinsic (or instrumental)? Opinions have been divided on the issue. On the one hand, supporters of a doctrine that we shall address again in Chapter 3, namely Formalism, have argued that the value of art is restricted to its structural balance and integrity, and so that it is entirely intrinsic. Art's value, this seems to say, is not only primarily intrinsic, but exclusively so: if we are ascribing to art one of the kinds of value discussed above, the Formalist holds, then we are ascribing the value to something other than the artwork. On the other hand, the contrary view – namely that the value of art is extrinsic – has one of its staunchest defenders in Tolstoy, for whom art is valuable only when it serves a moral or religious purpose.[8] For Tolstoy and other adherents to his view, then, art is held to be valuable only in so far as it yields some kind of moral or religious experience, or is the object of moral or religious contemplation, or is otherwise performative of some moral or religious function. For art to have value at all, on this account, it must have religious or moral value and therefore permits of extrinsic value only.

In less extreme cases, of course, we see that one object of artistic appreciation may well have both intrinsic *and* extrinsic value. A vase, for example, can have extrinsic value because of the relation it harbours to a particular collection of vases to which it belongs (it may be the most accomplished one of its kind, say). It may even have instrumental value in virtue of functioning unusually well as a holder for flowers. But none of that excludes the possibility that it may also have intrinsic value in virtue of its aesthetic features, and the general experience it gives rise to. On a simple view, then, just as art seems to allow for several kinds of value simultaneously, there are no *prima facie* reasons for considering that it cannot at the same time permit of both intrinsic and extrinsic value.

Nonetheless, the case for the claim that the value of art must first and foremost be considered as intrinsic seems worth pursuing when we consider art as art. That is to say, art may well have both intrinsic and extrinsic value, but *qua* art, it is the intrinsic value that seems to matter most – and not merely from a philosophical point of view. For when we value art, we value it primarily for its own sake: when I engage with a musical piece such as Chopin's G minor Ballade, I appreciate it primarily for the value of the experience independently of any relation it may bear to another experience. In other words, I listen to the rising and falling volume, the increase in intensity with each restatement of the main theme, the sense of release at the end, the sense of dramatic anticipation at the beginning, and I seem to do all this without necessarily inferring anything else on behalf of the work, such as its relation to Chopin's other pieces, or indeed to other performances of the same work. And, on the face of it at any rate, the fact that the work may have a value in terms of its documentary interest to musicologists, or from the fact that it discourages teenagers from loitering in Newcastle's underground system, seems irrelevant to my experience of the Ballade as a work of art in its own right.

It is here that the question of the value of the experience of art comes into closer focus. As we saw, that which seemed to underlie the phenomenon of the value of art was the way in which we experience it: our involvement with the artwork seems to be that which draws value from it. Having made the distinction between intrinsic and extrinsic value, however, it seems possible that we might best say that the aspect of experience seems to have more bearing when we are interested in the artwork for itself, self-evidently so if we happen to consider that art's intrinsic value consists in the kind of experience it affords. As Budd puts it,

> the work's artistic value is the intrinsic value of this experience. So a work of art is valuable as art if it is such that the experience it offers is intrinsically valuable; and it is valuable to the degree that this experience is intrinsically valuable. (1995: 5)

But what does a commitment to this point imply as far as the relation between aesthetic and artistic value is concerned? Certainly the Formalists, for whom the value of art is absolutely confined to a work's formal features and characteristics, hold it for true that the intrinsic value of art is exclusively to be cashed out in aesthetic terms. The formal features they are concerned with are distinctively aesthetic, and so it is a work's aesthetic qualities that contain the key to its intrinsic value *qua* art. Even the case described above of listening to Chopin's G minor Ballade is told by means of what is clearly an aesthetic experience. Is it the case, then, that the only value intrinsic to our experience of art is its aesthetic value?

Interestingly, when we centralize the element of experience in this way, what we understand by intrinsic value seems not only to comprise art's aesthetic value but also some of the other kinds of value we spoke of, perhaps, in particular, moral value. For it would seem that in order for us to ascribe cognitive or historical value to an artwork, we have no particular requirement to experience the artwork on its own terms – we may simply know *about* it, rather than know it in itself. But where a work yields moral value, say, it seems on the contrary that the element of experience is no less essential than in the aesthetic case. That *Carmen* leads us to side with its eponymous heroine and perhaps even question one's traditional moral sympathies is not only an aspect of the overall experience that the work affords that must be experienced directly, but also part of why we value the opera for its own sake. It is, in other words, part of why the *experience* of the artwork is intrinsically valuable.[9]

Once reached, this position helps us to make sense of how certain non-aesthetic kinds of value undeniably do seem to be part of the intrinsically valuable experiences we have of art: aesthetic value is not, in other words, the only kind of value of art that yields intrinsically valuable experience. This aspect of artistic experience is perhaps particularly apparent in Conceptual Art, which specifically aims not to have aesthetic value but which can lead us to undergo intrinsically valuable artistic experiences nonetheless. What is more, unless one defines the category of art in a manner that relies on the very point under scrutiny here (i.e. that art must be aesthetically valuable to be art), one must admit that art is not always a term of aesthetic praise. That is to say, art can be art without being good or valuable from an aesthetic point of view, which clearly indicates that the two kinds of value can come apart.

To the question of what the value of art actually amounts to, then, we may say the following. First, the value of art can reasonably be held to be constituted by different kinds of value. Particularly pertinent to the intrinsically valuable experience of art in this respect are aesthetic and moral value. Second, since that which makes the experience of art intrinsically rewarding is not exclusively its aesthetic qualities, aesthetic and artistic value cannot be said to be one and the same. The value of art is thus best understood in terms of its rewarding experience, and how that experience is to be explained is the main theme of Part II.

PRELIMINARY CONCLUSIONS: MORAL, AESTHETIC AND ARTISTIC VALUE

Once the class of potential objects of aesthetic appreciation and assessment is narrowed down to the smaller category of artworks, the threefold distinction between aesthetic, moral and artistic value becomes apparent. For unless one specifically takes the view that two of the three overlap completely – be it aesthetic and artistic value, or aesthetic and moral value, or again artistic and moral value – even a brief examination of these kinds of value reveal fundamental differences that separate them from one another quite plainly.

Unsurprisingly, aesthetic value is the kind of value that a particular artwork can be said to have in virtue of its aesthetic qualities (such as balance, ugliness, serenity or gracefulness). Similarly, moral value is that worth which can be ascribed to a work because of its moral content and character (for example, a painting may represent a cruel or just scene, or a novel may present its characters or their actions as virtuous or vicious). Artistic value, then, is the value yielded by an artwork's overall artistic character. If aesthetic, moral, or any other kind of value contributes (more or less directly) to the value of a work *qua* art, then, it is a part of what we have in mind when we refer to a work's overall artistic value. Artistic value thus encapsulates aesthetic and moral value under the condition that they participate in the work's overall value when considered as art. It is, in other words, always or necessarily the case that aesthetic or moral value is part of a work's intrinsic value.

In addition to highlighting the many kinds of value that can be ascribed to art, the main aim of this chapter has been to isolate aesthetic and moral value as two kinds of value that are often particularly pertinent to a work's intrinsic value. As we shall see in the next chapter, however, there is a further kind of value that calls for our attention in so far as it reveals something important about the philosophical scope and depth of a work's moral value. Although this may, in some respects, be seen to represent a slight deviation from our main theme, it will bring us closer to a good understanding of how powerful the influence that moral value may have on artistic appreciation in general and aesthetic appreciation in particular can be. This will equip us to address head-on the question of the extent to which moral value influences artistic assessment in Chapter 4 and, eventually, that of especially problematic cases in Chapter 5.

PART II

ART AND MORAL VALUE

CHAPTER 3

ART AS A SOURCE OF UNDERSTANDING

THE COGNITIVE VALUE OF ART

Of the many kinds of value we may ascribe to art, one is perhaps particularly controversial in so far as many philosophers have disputed both its significance and benefit to artworks. Cognitive value, it has thus been held, has no place in our experience of art, and should be considered neither a valid aim nor a criterion for good art. Instead, some have argued, art should set out to express or arouse emotion. On this line, then, the role of art is to induce *affective* – not *cognitive* – experience. To promote an agenda whereby knowledge and understanding is part of why we value art is, supporters of such Emotivism and Expressivism argue,[1] to misunderstand the role of art and, moreover, to distort its very nature.

At a first glance, this may seem a peculiar position to hold for at least two reasons. First, cognitive value seems to be a kind of value that artworks have in virtue of having some other, say, emotional, historical or political value. In other words, the claim that art can enrich our life through other than directly affective channels often rests on artistic features that are not primarily cognitive themselves. For example, and as we have already mentioned, Picasso's *Guernica* seems to have cognitive value at least partly because of its emotional content: the work yields insight and knowledge not only of the Spanish Civil War and how it was conducted by its military leaders, but also, and more generally, about the human suffering that ensues from political conflict. One concern with this approach in particular, or the denial of cognitive value for art in general on the grounds that art is primarily and exclusively about yielding aesthetic pleasure or sentiment, thus lies with what may be considered a misguided conception of the way in which the kinds of value art can have interact and depend upon one another.

Second, while art is obviously capable of generating pleasurable feelings – such as feeling weightless when looking at an elegant sculpture or enjoying a harmonious combination of colours in a painting – these enjoyable sentiments are at least at times ancillary to the principal value of the artwork, or at least not all there is to its overall worth. As we saw in the opening of Chapter 2, many artworks are capable of yielding valuable experiences that last longer, are more widely applicable, and may be more meaningful than this kind of pleasure. What is more, artworks seem able to enhance and add depth to our life by increasing our general awareness and intensifying the development of our perceptual and interpretative skills.

Prominent among those philosophers who defend the view that cognitive value is not only possible with regards to art but actually important to our understanding of it, is Aristotle. In his *Poetics*, he writes that poetry treats of universals (or concepts) rather than particulars, and is an excellent vehicle for transmitting knowledge of the former. Art, for Aristotle, is thus the realization of a universal: unlike history, which is limited to listing past events and is thus constrained to particulars, art seeks to capture and portray the universal in each individual phenomenon. Recently, and as we shall soon see in greater detail, Martha Nussbaum (1990) has built on this Aristotelian approach and argued that great works of literature necessarily deepen our moral understanding and development. They do so, Nussbaum explains, by focusing our attention and shaping our attitudes appropriately.

To put it simply, then, one of the main reasons why one might value art on the Aristotelian approach is that it seems to enhance our life by yielding some form of understanding, insight and knowledge that we deem important both in relation to ourselves and to our fellow human beings. However, since not everyone agrees with this claim, and some of the objections that have been raised against it do *prima facie* seem both convincing and solid, let us turn to assess its validity.

Before embarking on such an investigation, however, it is important to note that there are actually two – rather than one – concerns to address here: first, there is the question of whether art really is capable of yielding cognitive experiences of the kind required for the claim that art can have substantial cognitive value; second, there is the issue that even if art is indeed capable of yielding such experiences and thus of having substantial cognitive value, the kind of value in question here is not relevant to the overall value of art.

The first point finds an early expression in Plato's *Republic*, where it is held that even though imitative art purports to give us knowledge, it in actual fact only produces a deceptive appearance of knowledge. As we saw in Chapter 1, Plato held that the grounding of artistic practice in a principle that answered ultimately to pleasure rather than to rational understanding discounted any claims art might have to yield knowledge. The absence of an intelligible Form of, or a fully rational principle for, the idea of art, in other words, prevents that which it seeks to convey from being assessed in a manner appropriate to the idea of knowledge.

In a similar vein, yet much more recently, it has been held that avant-garde art cannot yield any substantial knowledge, since the representative means employed by such art are incapable of conveying any cognitive content worthy of the name. Such art, it has been argued, may only appeal to that which is already widely known, thus acting simply as a kind of reminder (albeit often a forceful one) of knowledge previously acquired. All that avant-garde art may yield, then, are truisms and clichés, and this is hardly material, it is held, for the ascription of genuine cognitive value.[2]

The second question has perhaps most eagerly been pressed by Formalists, such as Clive Bell, who emphasize the importance of aesthetic form to the detriment and even exclusion of any other feature that an artwork may have. On this view, a work's formal qualities single-handedly determine that work's value as art. Clearly, for Formalists, the (only) kind of artistic value that is fundamental to art and our conception of its worth is aesthetic value, where such value is defined purely in terms of beautiful formal qualities. As we established in Chapter 2, only beautiful form is salient to the value of art if Formalists are to be believed.

Interestingly, these two concerns need not go hand in hand or even mutually endorse one another. For Formalists can allow that art has the ability to give us some understanding and knowledge even though they maintain that that knowledge is of no consequence whatsoever to our appreciation and assessment of the artwork as such. Thus it would seem that at the very least we have some room to manoeuvre here. This scope for flexibility will serve us well in this, and the two chapters to come. For the general aim of Part II is to examine three concerns that are not only very interesting in their own right, but also prepare the ground for a detailed investigation into the philosophical relation between beauty and moral goodness at a rather more conceptual level.

Let us begin by looking at the main arguments both for and against the claim that art can yield knowledge in general, in order eventually to home in on the issue of whether it can, or cannot, give us moral knowledge in particular. The outcome of this question will have wide-ranging ramifications for our underlying concern in the relation between Aesthetics and Morality since many aspects of the suggestion that aesthetic and moral value can exercise mutual influence on one another depends on the possibility that art can indeed yield some form of moral knowledge or understanding. The arguments presented by those who wish to reject Cognitivism in general, usually called 'Non-Cognitivists', are philosophically significant not only in virtue of capturing concerns that, at least at a first glance, seem to have a lot of intuitive force, but also for what they reveal about Cognitivism.

COGNITIVISM: FOR AND AGAINST

The positive view best known as the doctrine of Cognitivism is centred around two main tenets: first, that art is capable of giving us non-trivial knowledge; second, that a work's cognitive value crucially determines its overall value as art. Interestingly, after several decades of Formalist and Emotivist orthodoxy, the tide recently seems to have turned to the advantage of Cognitivism. One reason for this change might be that the main idea underlying the doctrine has been given various expressions and turned into several more specific theories that do not overlap in every respect. This development has widened the spectrum of applicability for Cognitivism and thereby increased the possibilities for defending itself. As a result, at least some of the more recent versions of the doctrine of Cognitivism seem to manage to dodge the bullets directed at it by its opponents.

The arguments levelled against Cognitivism can, roughly, be divided into two main kinds, each corresponding to the two tenets outlined above: (i) arguments that set out to undermine the idea that art can yield knowledge that may rightly be described as substantial and meaningful; and (ii) arguments that target the very possibility of art's yielding knowledge in the first place. Let us examine these challenges by looking at two ways of defending (i) and (ii) respectively.

One way to challenge the epistemological standing of the knowledge that may be given to us through art centres around the genuine difficulty of stating exactly what it is we learn from experiencing art. For to recount precisely what knowledge one can gain from reading Flaubert's *Madame Bovary* or contemplating Manet's *The Execution of the Emperor Maximilian*, for example, is not an easy task. If any concise answer is available to Cognitivists at all, Non-Cognitivists such as Jerome Stolnitz argue, it can only be expressed in very prosaic terms; the knowledge that Cognitivists claim to have gained can thus only be banal and insignificant. What is more, Stolnitz propounds, even if we were to grant to Cognitivism that it is possible to learn from our experiences of art, there is nothing about that knowledge that is unique to art – there are 'no distinctive artistic truths' (1992: 191–2). That is to say, the alleged knowledge could just as well be gained from other experiences, thereby rendering the idea of art as a source of understanding and knowledge completely superfluous.

The obvious place for the Cognitivist to start her riposte to this interpretation of (i) lies with the claim that although it certainly may, at least at times, be difficult to find the words to express exactly what one has learnt from experiencing a particular work of art, Cognitivism need not stand and fall with the claim that the knowledge in question here can be (entirely) captured in propositional terms. In this vein, David Novitz (1987) has held that the most important kind of knowledge that we stand to gain from art is, in actual fact, practical knowledge. For what we learn from acquainting ourselves with the character of Emma Bovary and from being guided through her thought-processes by Flaubert, cannot be exhausted by a mere statement such as 'Appearances are not always what they seem'. That is to say, what we can learn from a work such as *Madame Bovary* may not be safely encapsulated by propositions alone, but that does not automatically pose a problem for the Cognitivist since there is no need for her to posit that all, or even the most meaningful, knowledge that art may yield can be formulated in that way. Instead, it can be argued, we come to understand how easy it can be to be taken in by a person who seems kind-hearted and unselfish but who, in reality, is entirely self-serving and cold; we learn that there is both good and evil in all of us by being at least superficially duped by this seemingly loveable character that is Emma. The Cognitivist has the resources, then, to argue that even though it may be true that *some propositional knowledge* yielded by art is indeed banal, it does not follow that *all knowledge* yielded by art is either propositional or banal.

In the light of the above, the second way of arguing against the claim that art can yield non-trivial knowledge – namely, that even if art can have cognitive value then that knowledge may equally well be gained through other means – becomes even less threatening to the Cognitivist cause. For while some Cognitivists, such as Martha Nussbaum (1990), have held that the knowledge yielded by literary art is unique, it is possible to defend a version of the doctrine that is not committed to this claim. The knowledge that we stand to gain from art, it can be held, need not necessarily be available to us only through experiencing art. Perhaps, then, we could have learnt that which we learnt from Flaubert's character Emma Bovary by meeting such a person in our real life and being subjected to her egotistical outlook and ambitions. There may, in that sense, be no distinctively 'artistic truth' to be uncovered here. But that concession does not in itself detract from the claim that such knowledge may *also* be gained through art. In real life, one may well add, we are often too directly involved to draw the appropriate lessons from our experiences. However, when we engage with a literary artwork such as *Madame Bovary* we have the adequate distance required in order fully to grasp the insight and knowledge that can be yielded by the situation.

All in all, then, it seems that (i), or arguments that set out to undermine the idea that art can yield knowledge that may rightly be described as substantial and meaningful, do not succeed in undermining the doctrine of Cognitivism as such, for at least some Cognitivisms can make room and accommodate for the concerns highlighted by the two versions of (i) examined here. Nussbaum's theory may not be capable of incorporating the Non-Cognitivist's commitment to the non-uniqueness of knowledge gained through literary art, but, as we have seen, other more moderate versions of Cognitivism can allow for such a claim. Similarly, all Cognitivism requires in order to refute the first version of (i) is to show that propositional knowledge is not the only kind of knowledge that art can yield, and this thought is so widely held among Cognitivists that the Non-Cognitivist objection simply seems to misfire in this respect. Cognitivism, or at least some versions of it, can survive this set of accusations.

The second line of argument that has been developed against Cognitivism concerns the logical possibility of art's alleged ability to yield knowledge. For on the first version of (ii), it is held that in order for knowledge of the real (i.e. non-fictional) world to be imparted through art, art must refer to that world. However, and as Terry Diffey (1995) has argued, art conspicuously fails to do so. What art does instead is to invite us into a world that is imaginary and therefore has no genuine bearing on the actual world that we live in from day to day. The beauty of art is that it remains within the confines of our imagination. Art, in other words, simply cannot breach that logical distance between these two worlds (i.e. real and fictional) epistemologically speaking.

This objection seems unconvincing for two reasons. First, and rather obviously, not all art is fictional. Although *Madame Bovary* clearly is the work of Flaubert's imagination, *The Execution of the Emperor Maximilian* does not depict a fictional event. Emperor Maximilian really was executed by a Republican firing squad on 19 June 1867 in the state of Querétaro just north of Mexico City. Second, even with regards to artworks that do not refer to a real event, person or place, it is not obvious that the assumption underlying Diffey's argument is valid, namely that only that which directly refers to the real world can have direct cognitive bearing on that world. Why, one may wonder, would sufficient similarity between one fictional and one non-fictional case not suffice? After all, although Emma Bovary herself might never have existed, it is almost certain that persons like her have, do and will exist in reality. Indeed, it could be argued, having read Flaubert's novel we stand a greater chance of coming to know those who in real life show similarities with Emma Bovary, and may alter our actions and judgements accordingly.

Along similar lines, another argument to the effect that art cannot actually yield knowledge emphasizes that knowledge is not only a matter of content but of the reliability of the method too: in order to have knowledge we may have to hold true beliefs, but those beliefs must also be justifiable, reliable and not merely acquired by chance. Art, Stolnitz (1992) has argued, cannot fulfil this condition, for beliefs acquired through art can never count as evidence. For that reason, Non-Cognitivists argue, it is not possible for art to yield knowledge that is relevant and applicable to the real world.

Again, this accusation seems to rest on an overly narrow conception of knowledge and understanding. While it is certainly true that for a belief to qualify as knowledge it must be possible to justify that belief, it need not be the case that the justification of that belief (albeit about a fictional event, person or situation) cannot appeal to facts and features of the real world. If the situation, person or event described in the artwork is sufficiently similar to a situation, person or event in the real world, then there is no particular reason why we could not ground the knowledge yielded by the artwork in reality. In fact, so doing is not merely desirable but actually necessary if the knowledge and understanding given to us through art is to have any bearing on our life. Several Cognitivists are thus ready to allow for the claim that art can never yield comprehensive knowledge of an event, person or place in real life. Hilary Putnam (1978), for example, grants that literary artworks can never give us knowledge of what actually occurred at a particular place and time. What is more, knowledge yielded by art can never withstand 'scientific testing' in the way that most other forms of knowledge can. However, what *is* of importance to the Cognitivist is that art can yield knowledge of possibilities – albeit that those possibilities are sometimes realized and sometimes not.

Having thus rejected the main arguments levelled against Cognitivism, let us now turn to an examination of the kinds of knowledge that art may yield. For it is not because art can be shown to be capable of yielding knowledge in general that it may be assumed to yield moral knowledge as such. It is, in other words, a further question whether art can be a source of moral understanding – one we shall turn to directly in the penultimate section of this chapter.

WHAT KINDS OF KNOWLEDGE CAN ART YIELD?

If Cognitivism is to be endorsed, the question immediately arises as to what *kind(s)* of knowledge art is capable of yielding? Providing a taxonomy of the different forms of knowledge that art may give will enable us to form a clearer idea of the many claims that

Cognitivism encapsulates, and, most importantly for our purposes, help us establish whether moral knowledge can in fact be gained from experiencing art. Of the several kinds of knowledge that Cognitivists have laid claim to, a handful of particularly interesting ones deserve special attention. At the risk of over-simplifying what are mostly very complex and sensitive theories, Cognitivists can be said to hold that art can be the source of four broad kinds of knowledge. These kinds do, in turn, take several forms.

First, and in a manner closely related to what was discussed at the end of the previous section, art can be said to give us conceptual knowledge of possible scenarios, be they past, present or future. In this vein Putnam has maintained that a novel such as Doris Lessing's *The Golden Notebook* can give us insight and understanding into what would be involved in being confronted with the dilemmas raised by a commitment to Communism during the 1940s. In addition, the work tells us about these concerns from a feminist perspective. What Lessing manages to achieve, Putnam argues, is to represent 'a certain moral perplexity' or problem that 'might have been felt by one perfectly possible person in a perfectly definite period' (1978: 489). In a nutshell, then, what Putnam is suggesting 'is that if we want to reason rationally about feminism, communism, liberalism, or just about life in the twentieth century, then what Doris Lessing does for our sensibility is enormously important' (1978: 489). From art we can thus gain understanding and insight into situations we might not ourselves have experienced directly.

Closely related to this form of knowledge, and even more directly connected with our previous discussion, it has been held that art can give us knowledge not only about what is possible but what is actual. In relation to the point examined above about whether knowledge of the real world, to be imparted through art, must refer to that world, Novitz (1987) has defended the view that literary artworks can give us knowledge of what is actually the case in the real world. By leading us to form new and original combinations of ideas, our imagination is said to contribute to generating hypotheses that can be deemed reliable even though they do not directly result from real events themselves. To use one of Novitz's own examples, if, in response to Dostoevsky's *Crime and Punishment*, 'one believes that human selfishness is frequently lost in times of ordeal', then 'one may come to think of ordeals not just as a threat to human life and limb, but as a way of overcoming one's self-centredness' (1987: 137). Clearly, the claim that art can give us this kind of understanding directly contradicts Diffey's idea, discussed in the previous section, that art can never yield knowledge of anything beyond the remit of its own fictional world.

A second, more practical, kind of knowledge that Cognitivists claim that art can yield is phenomenal by nature. This is a knowledge of what it is like to be, say, consumed by sexual jealousy, wrongly punished for a crime one didn't commit, devoted to a dying relative, or prone to suffer from stage-fright. Art, as Dorothy Walsh has explained, can widen our span of experiences and give us some form of epistemic access to situations, events and persons that we have not yet, or never will, experience first-hand (Walsh 1969). For example, although at least the great majority of us never have or ever will undergo Elizabeth Bennet's frustration at living in a society where marriage is the only path in life available to a young woman of a certain social standing, we can learn something about how deeply disappointing and terribly exasperating it would be to find oneself locked into such an unfair situation from reading Jane Austen's *Pride and Prejudice*. By engaging with artworks, then, we may 'stretch', so to speak, the knowledge that we have gained from our own experiences to cover sufficiently similar experiences that we have not ourselves undergone, thereby increasing our general understanding and knowledge of the world.

Further, art may teach us to assess the import and significance of certain events, persons or situations. We may, in other words, come to see that some particular aspect of a conversation, say, or one specific act, merits a reaction or response that we may not have ascribed to it had we been active participants in that act or dialogue ourselves. As R. W. Beardsmore (1973) has pointed out, literary artworks can, and often do, help us to recognize or find meaning in events or situations that we had originally not perceived at all, or perceived as meaningless. So while we might normally have taken it for granted that a particular friend would always adapt her plans to suit ours, reading a short story, say, in which a similar situation is described could help us understand the depth and effects of that friend's sacrifice. Art, in other words, can enhance our ability to see a certain situation or event for what it is worth, and so to judge it (or the sort of response it deserves) accordingly.

Third, art can be said to give us a form of practical knowledge that enables us to refine not merely our assessments, judgements and perceptions, but also other mental sensibilities and skills. Thus Jenefer Robinson (1995) has shown how engaging with art can refine and develop our emotions, by teaching us what kind of emotional response a certain situation or event might call for. A deep and genuine indignation is thus the appropriate emotion with which we ought to respond to the situation of Elizabeth Bennett even though her life is nearly exclusively filled with enjoyable events and concerns such as balls, dresses, walks in the countryside, and music-making. Similarly, we may learn from contemplating Manet's *The Execution of the Emperor Maximilian* not only how humiliating it must be for a head of state to be executed in such a summary fashion, but also how deeply unpleasant and uncomfortable it would be to witness such a scene even as an innocent bystander.

Intimately linked to this account is Gregory Currie's (1998) claim that art can actually enhance the way in which our imagination operates, thereby increasing our understanding not only of the sequence, structure and development of our own thoughts, but also augmenting our insight into how other persons think and reason. Generally speaking, experiencing artistic narratives (be it in films, novels or operas) teaches us to impose a certain kind of structure onto our own lives by helping us to pick out salient features that, in turn, enable us to make sense of the events, thoughts or decisions that we have set in motion. More specifically, engaging with imaginary characters may enable us to get closer both emotionally and intellectually to persons in real life.

Fourth, and most importantly for our purposes, some Cognitivists have held that art can yield a kind of conceptual knowledge which is first and foremost moral. Literature, in particular, it has frequently been held, can give its audience an invaluable form of knowledge of the nature of our moral concepts. Not only can we acquire or refine concepts with moral content, such as empathy and forgiveness, we can also come to adhere to an entire moral perspective and value-system. Eileen John (1998) has thus argued that a literary artwork, through inviting us to become intimate with characters we might never have met in our real life, say, can teach us to exercise sympathy in our interpretation of others and their actions. In a similar fashion, Nussbaum (1990) has held that while moral philosophy is capable of giving us an 'outline' of the good life, we need the kind of moral vision that is embodied in works of literature in order to fully grasp the particular requirements of individual situations. The literary arts are, then, crucial, not least for the way in which they complement our philosophizing about moral action and deliberation.

The claim that art can yield moral knowledge thus implies that art can give us a kind of knowledge that is, roughly, philosophical by nature. By that I do not mean to suggest that the moral knowledge that art may yield should be thought of as a *necessary* complement to moral philosophy or even a kind of philosophical exploration in its own right. Nevertheless, it is a knowledge based on an analysis that would appear to have aims or content of a broadly conceptual nature. For the moral knowledge that art can yield is one that can not only help us to enhance our grasp of moral concepts, but also increase our understanding of how we should relate to others, and what the primary goals and concerns of our life should be. We may, for example, come to a good understanding of the kind of person one should *not* aim to be by reading *Crime and Punishment* or looking at Hogarth's *Rake's Progress*. Conversely, we may derive and amplify our conceptions of concrete virtues by reading Dickens' *Bleak House*, or by listening to Händel's *Alcina*.

At least at a first glance, the span of moral knowledge that art is capable of yielding seems limitless. There seems to be no area of life, no kind of subject of experience, or indeed any element of thought that lies beyond the remit of the moral knowledge we stand to gain from art. But this is a bold suggestion to make, and one that carries considerable consequences for several aspects of the relation between Aesthetics and Morality. Is this really so, one must thus ask, and if not, what exactly are the boundaries of the ways in which a work's moral character can influence its artistic and aesthetic value?

THE SCOPE OF MORAL KNOWLEDGE YIELDED BY ART

Once the claim that art can yield moral knowledge has been accepted, it is important to reflect on what that view actually entails. For even when it has been agreed that Cognitivism may take a moral expression, the claim allows for differences of interpretation both with regards to scope and depth. Views on the matter range from the position that art may indeed indirectly yield some (albeit relatively weak) moral lesson to the stance that art is absolutely crucial to our moral understanding and education, and thereby central to our development as human beings. Further, whereas some theories hold that the moral knowledge and hence value that art can yield is entirely autonomous of the other kinds of value that it may have, others conceive of moral value as deeply intertwined with, especially, aesthetic value.

The aim of this section is to sketch two of the most interesting approaches to the question of the scope of moral knowledge. So doing will eventually enable us to tackle the second question, which is a recurrent theme of Chapters 4 and 5, equipped with a good understanding of the underlying debate and alternatives on offer. For the scope that we are willing to concede to the moral knowledge yielded by art will partly determine our conception of what art should aim to achieve, and thus, what art can bring to our life on the whole.

One theory already mentioned, namely Nussbaum's Cognitivist account, centres around the claim that literary artworks are fundamental to moral philosophy in particular, and life in general. Nussbaum writes that 'certain literary texts' are simply 'indispensable to a philosophical enquiry in the ethical sphere' and constitute 'sources of insight without which the enquiry cannot be complete' (1990: 23–4). What is more, 'certain truths about human life can only be fittingly and accurately stated in the language and forms characteristic of the narrative artist' (1990: 5). But how, one may ask, do novels, short stories and poems manage this impressive feat on Nussbaum's account?

Nussbaum holds that reading good literary artworks (novels especially) provides us with rich and appropriately complex concrete situations that encourage us to reflect on the moral content of such situations and sharpen our moral thought about similar cases. That is to say, literature urges – and actually enables – us to be more perceptive and sensitive to particular events, to be more discerning of all the features salient to a specific state of affairs, and to assess the response that an individual case calls for, more astutely. These skills, Nussbaum argues, are precisely those abilities that we need to employ in moral understanding. First and foremost, then, reading good literary works helps us develop the kind of sensitivity that is essential to moral understanding, and can thereby be said to yield a moral knowledge that is crucial to both moral deliberation and philosophical reflection.

Clearly, Nussbaum's theory counts among the staunchest supporters of the idea that (literary) art can yield robust and powerful moral knowledge. As explained above, one may even say that this account fails to represent the great majority of Cognitivists because of the twofold claim that art can yield solid propositional knowledge and that that knowledge is unique to art (i.e. can only be given to us through art). One commentator wishing to point out that Nussbaum exaggerates the possible strength of moral knowledge, Christopher Hamilton, has recently argued that Nussbaum's claims – for example to the effect that a novel always 'promotes mercy through its invitation to empathic understanding . . . and cultivates a moral ability that is opposed to hatred in its very structure' (2003: 40) – overstate the scope of the moral knowledge that art can sensibly yield. For Hamilton, it is simply not accurate to claim that reading a good novel invariably contributes to a virtuous and compassionate understanding of the particular person or situation described. Citing George Eliot's *Middlemarch* as an example, Hamilton endorses the idea that one might at times be inclined to aggressive and morally reprehensible attitudes towards fictional characters (2003: 40). Moreover, Hamilton continues, even if we were to grant that a good novel can encourage a compassionate view of the individual and thereby contribute to the refinement of our moral sensibility and understanding, there is still a question of whether that view of the particular person or situation described is one that we would want to promote.

A considerably more modest account of the way in which art may give rise to some moral understanding is one centred around the idea that literary (or narrative) art may clarify and expand the moral knowledge that we already possess. The suggestion is that although art cannot yield 'new propositional [moral] knowledge', engaging with art can 'deepen our moral understanding by, among other things, encouraging us to apply our moral knowledge and emotions to specific cases'. In the words of Noel Carroll,

[i]n the course of engaging with a given narrative we may need to reorganize the hierarchical orderings of our moral categories and premises, or to reinterpret those categories and premises in the light of new paradigm instances and hard cases, or to reclassify barely acknowledged phenomena afresh. (1998a: 142)

This may not constitute particularly strong or indeed unique moral knowledge, but, nonetheless, allows for the claim that literary art may cultivate and extend our grasp of moral concepts and enable us to make new connections among our moral beliefs.

In contrast to Nussbaum's account, this claim may, in turn, seem a little too meek and unassuming. For it is one thing to say that art can help us clarify pre-existing moral knowledge, and quite another to retract from more positive claims altogether, and hold that this is the *only* kind of moral understanding that art can unreservedly be said to yield. So, in view of being significantly less demanding than most other accounts, the question for Carroll's theory now becomes whether it is, in fact, demanding enough. For although it does seem difficult to defend Nussbaum's claim that literary works can be 'indispensable to a philosophical enquiry into the ethical sphere' (1990: 23), it does seem correct to hold that art can enable us to develop the kind of sensitivity that is central to moral understanding, and that certain literary works can constitute very valuable 'sources of insight' (1990: 24) which, at least at times, complement our philosophical enquiry very nicely. It may be natural that the relation between philosophical enquiry and good artwork is difficult to formalize. To use the words of Eileen John,

[w]e finish some works of fiction with the sense that they are extremely 'philosophical', but it is not easy to say what we mean by that. Presumably we mean various things: perhaps that the work of fiction is a work of philosophy that presents a philosophical position, or that the work implicitly assumes an interesting philosophical position, or that it is about a philosophical issue, or that it reveals philosophical dimensions to human life, or that the work has made us think philosophically. (1998: 331)

The accurate account to be given about the scope of art's moral knowledge seems to lie somewhere between the two positions examined in this section: through our experience of art we may acquire independent moral knowledge (i.e. not simply a clearer idea of a specific moral concept) even though that moral knowledge may not automatically represent a necessary component of our philosophizing about the moral concern in question.

Clearly, the enormous variety of the kinds of experience we derive from artworks – even simply from literature – is going to be a problem for any account that attempts to present a unified theory of the kind of knowledge that can be drawn from them. There are, for example, many works of literature that are almost completely amoral in content. Georges Perec's *La Disparition*, for example, seems to be about nothing other than the intellectual pleasure of contemplating the peculiar form of the novel itself, and, by extension, the relation that form bears to the idea of literature as a whole. But many if not most of the subjects addressed by novels are specifically moral in nature, or at least partly so; and where some seem to call for Carroll's weaker account, for others one would want to appeal squarely to something more substantial, closer to the line drawn by Nussbaum. For while one might argue that it is impossible to understand *Anna Karenina* without already having the appropriate moral concepts of hypocrisy, shame, vanity and self-destruction, Carroll would allow that the representation of these concepts in an aesthetically compelling fashion gives psychological weight to them in a way that *almost* constitutes discovering them anew. But for other cases, such as, for example, Daniel Defoe's *Robinson Crusoe*, many of the moral questions and precepts represented are so rooted in the context of total physical isolation that it would seem impossible to have knowledge of them without having read that particular book or another similar one. Then again, the uniqueness claim at the centre of Nussbaum's theory does seem difficult to uphold in connection with any widely accepted conception of what it is to know something.

It is interesting to note, moreover, that although Nussbaum's account obviously recommends a strong interpretation of the scope of the moral knowledge that art can yield, and Carroll's suggestion builds on the weaker idea that art can develop and intensify the morally laden concepts and beliefs that we already have, both theories have strong implications with regards to the moral assessment of art. For once we start thinking about the extent to which our moral convictions should be allowed to influence our general artistic assessments, we begin to see that the question about the scope addressed in this section acquires a dimension that pervades our interaction with much of art.

PRELIMINARY CONCLUSIONS:
ART AS A SOURCE OF MORAL UNDERSTANDING

The principal concern of this chapter has been to examine whether, and if so how, art can be a source of moral knowledge and understanding and thereby shed some light on one manner in which moral value may influence artistic appreciation. For if a work's moral content or character can yield knowledge – and so have both moral and cognitive value – then this is definitely going to be relevant to that work's intrinsic value.

Many theories and philosophical approaches either ignore or set out to disprove the idea that art should in any way aspire to yield knowledge and understanding of any kind, let alone moral knowledge. As we have seen, Formalists, Emotivists and no doubt others hold that cognitive and moral character is neither here nor there in so far as artistic appreciation and assessment is concerned. Nevertheless, it has been argued that reasons for endorsing Cognitivism outweigh any grounds one might have for setting non-cognitive content and character in exclusive focus in artistic appreciation. Further, and as we shall soon see, the possibility of moral knowledge is central to some aspects of our account of moral value in relation to aesthetic value too.

The idea that we stand to gain moral lessons or improved moral concepts as a result of engaging appropriately with artworks is presupposed by many of the theories to which we shall turn our attention in Part III. Regardless of whether one endorses those theories or not, however, the discussion in the present chapter will help us understand one of the main ways in which moral knowledge and understanding need not always take a purely propositional form. One of the things we may learn from art with moral content, then, is something more fundamental about what it really is to be a morally good person, and, generally speaking, the kind of aims one ought to pursue to lead a good life.

CHAPTER 4

MORAL CONVICTIONS AND
ARTISTIC APPRECIATION

HOW DO WE APPRECIATE ARTWORKS?

The question of whether our moral convictions should influence our appreciation of artworks addresses the threefold relation between (i) our personal moral beliefs and commitments, (ii) an artwork's moral character, and (iii) a work's value *qua* art. In the first instance, there is an issue about whether (i) and (ii) can be separated to the extent that one can, in artistic appreciation, suspend a moral conviction to which one has a deep pre-existing commitment. That is to say, can artistic moral character on the one hand, and personal moral conviction on the other, be perceived as distinct and yet mutually endorsed in the appreciation of art? In the second instance, there is a parallel concern about whether (i) and (iii) can be separated in so far as a work's moral character may stimulate moral beliefs in us that, although relevant and appropriate to the work, directly clash with our personal moral convictions. The question then is whether we can sidestep and overlook our own convictions in the process of appreciating the work of art as art, and thus on its own terms.

Aristotle already understood that the problem raised by art with a moral character is a distinctively philosophical one: under scrutiny is not merely the everyday psychology of experiencing art with certain moral features but, rather, a conceptual issue about how moral value is, as a matter of definition, linked to the overall worth of art. Once this has been effectively established, it is possible to discern at least two important sets of questions. First, there is the notion of artistic appraisal and the extent to which moral value should determine artistic or aesthetic value. Second, there is the concern centred around whether art, to be good art, must serve a moral purpose. The answers Aristotle eventually offers in his *Poetics* are affirmative in both cases: the moral character of a particular work of art *can* be intimately linked to its value as art, and moral criteria *can* indicate which tragedies, say, are good or bad.

These two sets of questions will occupy the rest of Part II. In this chapter, we will focus on the first of these concerns, and examine the notion of moral value in relation to artistic appraisal and evaluation in particular cases. In the next chapter, we shall turn to an investigation of moral value in relation to artistic quality in general. Two broad approaches have dominated these debates. One school of thought denies that there can be any kind of internal philosophical relation between moral value and the value of art, and so that art must be assessed, be it in particular or general, solely in terms of its non-moral features. The other approach, however, holds the contrary view that the value of art must be conceived at least partly in terms of its moral value. As we shall see, in the process of exploring these two alternatives, we will have to remain vigilant not to confound aesthetic and artistic value for the reasons outlined towards the end of the previous chapter.

Let us begin by examining the question with regards to the way in which we judge and evaluate the individual artworks we come across in museums, libraries or concert halls. Should we let our moral beliefs influence our appreciation of them, or should we rather try to distance ourselves from our usual frame of reference?

AUTONOMISM AND AESTHETICISM

The view that the moral value of art is, as a matter of principle, independent of its other kinds of value can be read in different ways depending on how strongly one conceives of the independence in question. To Formalists such as Clive Bell, the moral character of a work is entirely irrelevant to its intrinsic artistic value, since, and as explained in the previous chapter, the only thing that is pertinent to artistic appraisal and evaluation is beautiful form (Bell 1914). Art is valuable, in other words, if and only if it has aesthetic value. Bell grounds this claim in the more far-reaching thought that *all* artistic content is simply beside the point when it comes to assessing and judging art. What we have to do instead is endorse something like what the psychologist Edward Bullough describes as 'psychical distance' towards art, that is to say, an attitude whereby we suspend our usual outlook on things in the world and instead adopt a manner of perception which separates 'the object and its appeal from one's own self, by putting it out of gear with practical needs and ends' (1912: 96).

This line of argument, generally referred to as Radical Autonomism or Simple Aestheticism, paints an unlikely picture of the relation between moral value and other values that art may have. Most importantly, the claim that all content is irrelevant to the evaluation of art seems highly implausible. Take the example of Grayson Perry's vases, say. These are delicately shaped, decorated in very pleasing colour combinations, and may therefore be said to have beautiful form. But it seems difficult if not impossible to maintain that position once we discover on closer inspection that the vases are covered with representations of scenes of child abuse and distorted images of children in general. Again, and less extremely, Tolstoy's *War and Peace* is a beautifully written work, peppered with wonderful descriptions of both fictional characters and situations. Nevertheless, the fact that some of the battle-scenes portrayed are depicted in an extremely long and detailed manner, seeming thereby to detract from the overall line of thought of the book, may be said to diminish its intrinsic value on occasion. In other words, artistic content does, albeit perhaps only obliquely and under certain circumstances, influence an artwork's aesthetic value. Such Radical Autonomism can be refuted even within an Autonomist framework for characterizing the independence of moral value in excessively strong terms.[1]

An account that remains committed to the independence of moral value in relation to the intrinsic value of art, yet presents a far more reasonable conception of that independence, goes by the name of Moderate Autonomism or Sophisticated Aestheticism. On this kind of theory, an artwork's moral character *may* influence its intrinsic value – where such value is conceived primarily if not exclusively in aesthetic terms – but does not do so necessarily. The main idea is that an artwork's moral character influences its value indirectly if and only if that moral character mars or promotes the work's aesthetically valuable features. For supporters of this kind of Autonomism or Aestheticism such as Monroe Beardsley (1958) and Peter Lamarque (1995), it would seem problematic to deem an artwork bad, say, on the grounds that its moral characterization fails to be 'true to life', for such an assessment is taken to be irrelevant to its intrinsic value as art. However, if a novel's theme is either uninteresting or badly developed on its own terms, for example, as a result (albeit indirect) of the moral character of a work, then we can say that the work's value *qua* art is lessened. In artistic appraisal, what really matters is whether works of art manage to develop the imagery, characters and theme in ways that we find aesthetically appealing and convincing.

To all intents and purposes, this theory captures an important aspect of the way in which we assess artworks: although there is one sense in which one might want to say that Perry's vases are beautiful, their moral content is so horrific that it does seem to mar the aesthetic qualities of the work, thereby affecting its intrinsic value. To hold the vases to be beautiful without reservation and not consider that beauty negatively affected by the theme of the depictions would be grossly inappropriate.

However, there seem to be at least two questions that might prove contentious for Sophisticated Aestheticism. First, and as Matthew Kieran has argued, it may be problematic always to keep a safe distance – safe, that is, from the perspective of Aestheticism – from the claim that moral character can *directly* influence the aesthetic qualities of a work. Appraisals of artworks to the effect that they are, to use Kieran's examples, banal, sentimental, shallow or nuanced do seem at least at times difficult to specify without appeal to considerations such as plausibility, insight and explanatory power.[2] This, it is suggested, indicates that it may be harder than first suspected to guarantee the looked-for separation between the cognitive considerations and aspects of our artistic experience that relate directly to the work's aesthetic character. In other words, it may prove tricky for the supporter of Sophisticated Aestheticism to preserve the key tenet of the theory, which is to allow for *indirect* influence of a work's moral character on its aesthetic qualities.

In addition to this concern, one source of disquiet for Sophisticated Aestheticism relates to the way in which we may resist engaging imaginatively with an artwork's moral character, perhaps especially if that character is reprehensible.[3] That is to say, certain artworks, in order to be fully appreciated aesthetically, require that we employ our imagination. However, it does not always seem possible to take on the imaginative perspective that the work invites us to assume. For example, when we watch a film such as Quentin Tarrantino's *Pulp Fiction* which unashamedly glorifies gratuitous violence, or Leni Riefenstahl's *Triumph of the Will* which advocates the Nazi regime's value-system and ideals, we might not want or even be able to entertain the attitude prescribed by the work.

At least at a first glance, these matters are difficult to resolve for the supporter of Sophisticated Aestheticism. First, there is the pressing question of how to draw a line between direct and indirect influence, and moreover, to establish with certainty that the claim that moral value can never influence our aesthetic assessments in the former way is generally valid without exception. Second, there is the worry about the possibility of engaging imaginatively with artworks that recommend an outlook that is deeply counter-intuitive to us, where such an engagement is central to the aesthetic appreciation of the work of art in question.

Despite being confronted with these serious challenges, Sophisticated Aestheticism does seem to be at an advantage with regards to at least one important aspect of our artistic experiences, namely the way in which it can, at least at times, be not only desirable but also quite fitting to focus on a work's beauty or purely aesthetic value. For Sophisticated Aestheticism does not need to deny that we can assess an artwork for both its moral and aesthetic character. What it rejects is the idea that our aesthetic assessments should always be influenced by the work's moral character. To reiterate the point made at the beginning of this chapter, it is the *internal relation* between two kinds of value that is in question here.

So, perhaps there are ways around the two main problems sketched above. In the first instance, it may be possible to avoid conflation of direct and indirect influence simply by being more careful in our evaluations, and by discarding imprudent assessments that fail to draw on and make use of this conceptual distinction. In the second instance, and as Michael Tanner (1994) has pointed out, one of the most unsettling yet interesting things that a good artwork can do is precisely to get us to assent (albeit temporarily and fictionally) to perspectives that we find morally reprehensible. For example, Vladimir Nabokov's *Lolita* is a great novel partly because it manages to unpack and introduce us to the manner in which the unquestionably culpable paedophile protagonist views his relationship with a 12-year-old girl. Cases such as these most probably indicate that although the phenomenon of imaginative resistance carries some philosophical weight against Sophisticated Aestheticism, it cannot reject it single-handedly.

We shall soon turn to examine whether there is any philosophical mileage in these suggestions, and whether Sophisticated Aestheticism can be strengthened. Perhaps the theory can even be shown to represent the best account available in this debate. Before determining this question, however, we need to examine the position centred around the denial of Aestheticism's principal tenet. Once this has been done, we will revisit this discussion better equipped to assess its philosophical validity.

MORALISM AND ETHICISM

In direct contrast to Autonomism and Aestheticism, the approach generally known as Moralism centres around the claim that the moral character of an artwork is pivotal to our appreciation and assessment of that work. As stated by Tolstoy (1930), this view advocates a conception whereby the work of art's value is entirely determined by its moral character. Formulated in weaker, and considerably more plausible terms, the approach stands for the idea that a moral flaw may count as an aesthetic flaw and vice versa (where an aesthetic flaw is conceived as part of an artwork's intrinsic value). This position, Moderate Moralism, can rightly be described as more credible since, unlike Tolstoy's Radical Moralism, it is capable of accounting for the fact that at least some art is good *despite* being morally vacuous or reprehensible. In the words of Noël Carroll,

> [m]oderate moralism maintains that in some instances a moral defect in an artwork can be an aesthetic defect, and that sometimes a moral virtue can count as an aesthetic virtue. This opposes the view of moderate autonomism which admits that artworks can be morally defective and morally bad for that reason, but then goes on to say that the moral badness of a work can never count as an aesthetic defect. (1998b: 419)

On this line, then, moral assessment is key to the general assessment and evaluation of artworks in so far as appreciating artworks requires us to recognize the moral character and features endorsed (both explicitly and implicitly) by the work and, moreover, to endorse and feel in sympathy with them ourselves. In this sense, a moral flaw may also be considered an aesthetic flaw when a situation somehow fails to elicit from us the appropriate moral response and where the prompting of such a response is an integral part of the work. So, for example, when Raskolnikov is particularly vindictive and aggressive towards an old lady in the opening of Dostoevsky's *Crime and Punishment*, behaviour which eventually leads to his killing her, responding in terms of shame and disgust on Raskolnikov's behalf forms an essential part of engaging and appreciating the work as it was designed. Were the book consistently to fail to elicit this response, then it seems we could justifiably speak of the scene as aesthetically, and thus artistically, flawed. Or if – as it commonly does – the novel succeeds in soliciting those emotional responses because of its moral perspective on Raskolnikov's actions (i.e. one in which such behaviour is rightly to be considered shameful and disgusting), then we should consider its moral character to be an aesthetic virtue too.

It is then possible, according to Moderate Moralism, for an artwork to have a morally reprehensible character without this necessarily being relevant to its value as art. For such a moral character only takes on importance in relation to our overall assessment when it somehow impedes our capacity to engage with the artwork or to respond to it appropriately. That is to say, while Moderate Moralism does allow for mutual influence between moral and aesthetic value, it does recognize that great art need not have any moral character at all to be good art (which is principally why it represents an improvement over a Radical Moralism such as that of Tolstoy).

Having said that, Moderate Moralism certainly has some problems of its own to address. First and foremost, it may be held against Carroll's theory that in reality it fails to make room for the possibility that the moral features of a work can play a direct role in its resulting artistic value. For while a work's ability to be absorbing or to elicit emotional responses from us is largely an aesthetic matter, the question of whether these processes may be aided and enriched by the soliciting of a defective moral perspective is a question of a different order. In other words, the claim that has not been established yet, even though the theory depends on it, is that an artwork's intrinsic value is internally linked to the emotional responses we have to the work's moral character. I may not, say, be able to respond with anything other than indignation and resentment at the conception of women prevalent in Boccaccio's *Decameron*, but this only indicates that I am probably not the best person to assess how good this literary work is as art – *not* that it is not any good at all. So, underlying this aspect of Carroll's argument is the worry that the only thing the theory shows is that sometimes we are not in a position to judge how good an artwork is because of our reaction to its moral character.

In addition, Moderate Moralism has to address another serious challenge that concerns the way in which the theory relies on the idea that art must succeed in its morally laden aim, for some works do fail in that aim and, surprisingly perhaps, are better artworks in virtue of it. One obvious kind of case for which this concern has bite is propaganda art in the form of posters and films, say. Such artworks can at least sometimes be better art precisely because of not succeeding in arousing the moral sentiment and outlook that would, under normal circumstances, be appropriate.[4] Yet, as both Eileen John and Daniel Jacobson have pointed out (John 2005 and Jacobson 2005), Carroll wants to establish that moral virtues and flaws can sometimes also be artistic virtues and flaws, but his account does not seem capable of accepting that a work's moral flaw can, as in the case of propaganda art, sometimes also be considered an aesthetic virtue.

This last set of questions raised by opponents of Moderate Moralism suggest that Carroll's theory may be too weak to account for precisely those kinds of cases which might lead one to favour the Moralist approach on the whole. There is, however, another contender within that school of thought with a stronger Moralist character. Based on the idea expressed by David Hume as early as in the eighteenth century that 'where vicious manners are described, without being marked with the proper characters of blame and disapprobation; this must be allowed to disfigure the poem, and to be a real deformity' (1965: 21–2), the theory known as Ethicism generally rests on the claim that a moral flaw in an artwork is necessarily an aesthetic one too. Most recently defended by Berys Gaut, Ethicism thus holds that:

> the ethical assessment of attitudes manifested by works of art is a legitimate aspect of the aesthetic evaluation of those works, such that, if a work manifests ethically reprehensible attitudes, it is to that extent aesthetically defective, and if a

work manifests ethically commendable attitudes, it is to that extent aesthetically meritorious. (1998: 182)

According to Gaut, then, a work can be good in one respect (it may, say, be graceful) while being bad in another (it may, for example, manifest some morally reprehensible proposition). A morally flawed work may thus still be good *qua* art, but its moral flaw does to that extent count against its intrinsic value. For Gaut, a work's aesthetic value is 'the value of an object *qua* work of art. That is to say, its artistic value' (1998: 183).

The main argument offered by Gaut in support of Ethicism is based on the notion of merited response, for Ethicism is said to be a theory about a work's manifestation of certain moral attitudes, where those attitudes are manifested in the responses they prescribe to their audience. So, when a particular artwork prescribes a certain response that is (by definition) intrinsically linked to that work's value as art, and where that response depends on ethical evaluation, the moral character of a work is always relevant to its value as art. When we form the opinion that the person, situation or event portrayed does not warrant the endorsement of the evaluation prescribed by the work, then the response it seeks from us is not merited and we can (as we often do) legitimately fail to respond as prescribed. In other words, when the merited response comes apart from the prescribed response, the work is, in that respect, a failure.[5]

As Carroll has pointed out, Ethicism supports the view that moral flaws, where they bear on the responses sought from us, will always be aesthetic flaws and that moral adequacy, wherever it bears on our responses, will always be an aesthetic virtue. Although Ethicism, just like Moderate Moralism, appeals to emotional responses in its account of artistic value, the former is clearly committed to a stronger internal relation between a work's moral character and its value as art. To use Carroll's words,

Gaut seems willing to consider virtually every moral defect in a work of art an aesthetic defect, where I defend a far weaker claim – namely that sometimes a moral defect in an artwork can count as an aesthetic defect, or, as Hume would say, a blemish. Thus you can see that ethicism is a very strong position, while mine is, well, moderate. (1998b: 419)

While Ethicism may certainly be considered an improvement on Moderate Moralism if one considers the relatively irregular relation between moral and artistic value to be a weakness in Carroll's theory, the argument of merited response upon which Ethicism relies has, however, given rise to several objections of its own. One theme that recurs in these accusations is that Gaut is too quick to draw aesthetic conclusions, or conclusions about the artwork's value as art, from the idea that a certain moral character may call for a specific emotional response. So, on the one hand, the argument has been portrayed as equivocating between aesthetic and moral value, and thus of being structurally unsound in virtue of starting off from a claim about ethical merit and ending up with a claim about aesthetic merit. Similarly, it has been held that the aesthetic defects of a work cannot be reduced to a failure of prescribed responses, for while some works clearly prescribe responses, not all do.

More importantly perhaps, John and Jacobson have highlighted the way in which the principal argument for Ethicism equivocates between notions of merited response. As John (2005) explains, the response that is merited by the artwork's manner of presenting a situation and the response merited by an independent moral assessment of that situation may or may not be the same, whereas it seems only to be the first kind that is obviously relevant to artistic value in Gaut's sense. And, as Jacobson (2005) has pointed out, it is one thing for an emotional response to be 'fitting' with respect to its object and another for it to be morally proper. What it is for an emotion to be fitting is for it to accurately present its object in terms of certain evaluative features. But from the fact that a response may not be morally right or proper it does not necessarily follow that a particular response is not fitting in the context of the work: indeed, it may well be part of a work's success – and here, *Lolita* is an obvious case in point – that it solicits responses that are immoral but still fitting.

Of the two theories within the Moralist approach, a first examination thus leaves us with no obvious frontrunner. Both theories have strengths and weaknesses, and the balancing act between these advantages and disadvantages awaits a closer scrutiny of certain problematic cases in order to be resolved. However, what is clear at this stage of our enquiry is that the question we started off by defining has slightly changed in meaning. For the query about

72

whether we should let our moral convictions influence our aesthetic appreciation and assessment has now turned into a concern about whether the moral character of the artwork should influence its intrinsic character as art. That is to say, the question is now less about the threefold relation we began by describing, and seems more directly concerned with an internal relation between two kinds of value legitimately ascribed to a particular artwork. Nevertheless, we will return to our original concern in Part III and reflect on how the relation between an artwork's moral character (ii) and that work's intrinsic value as art (iii) corresponds, if at all, to that which links our personal moral convictions (i) and a work's intrinsic value (iii).

EVALUATING THE ROLE OF MORAL ASSESSMENT: HARD CASES

It is now perfectly clear that the question that served as a starting-point to the present chapter's enquiry is a genuinely perplexing one. For not only do we discover a whole array of questions when we start unpacking our original concern, but we also find that there are serious advantages and disadvantages to both sides of the debate. So, what is one to conclude?

In favour of Aestheticism (certainly the Sophisticated version) is the way in which we at least at times are perfectly capable of distinguishing neatly between a work's moral character and its intrinsic value as art and, moreover, disregard the former in our overall assessment of that artwork. For it seems completely appropriate with regards to artworks such as the provocative and proud prostitute that Manet depicts in *Olympia* to pay no attention to the moral content and perspective imposed upon us by these works when we evaluate them. After all, even though some of us might find *Olympia*'s shamelessness and lack of modesty shocking, our assessment of the work *qua* art is generally not affected by its moral character, and nor perhaps should it be. What we are judging here is the way in which Manet has brought this girl to life, the elegance with which he has rendered her poise and personality, and the beauty of the moment that he has captured. These things, or so it seems, are not dependent on whether the girl in question is a prostitute or the proverbial vicar's daughter.

Then again, there are cases such as Perry's vases or Riefenstahl's

Triumph of the Will, where such a separation seems neither easy nor desirable. For it seems morally inadequate, at the very least, to say that the moral content of such works should be of no concern to us in the process of appreciating and assessing such artwork *qua* art. The experience of disgust, after all, appears to be central to the artistic experience of Perry's vases – take away this reaction and the vases are, well, just vases. Having said that, we are now equipped with a distinction that can help us here, because what is important in this process is the moral perspective offered – not necessarily the moral content as it may appear at a first glance – and this enables us to set aside the worry at least in relation to works such as Perry's. The moral perspective offered to us in these vases is precisely one that is *not* contrary to our own moral beliefs and convictions, namely that child abuse may be very difficult to detect, and can often hide behind a pleasant and nice façade, but that it is horrible nonetheless. Moreover, it raises the question among its perceivers of the moral responsibility of the bystander, who looks without really observing and taking in what she sees.

With the Riefenstahl case, on the other hand, we find a film that imposes an outlook with which we cannot possibly agree or to which we are morally bound to deny our sympathy. For what the director is offering to the mind is, after all, the very heart of Nazi ideology, heralded as true, beautiful and historically inevitable. It would seem that under no circumstances could our own present subscription to such a point of view be recommended.

Clearly, hard cases such as these are a crucial asset to the Moralist camp, for it is very difficult for the Autonomist or Aestheticist to retain their credibility in the light of works with such morally reprehensible character. Of course, Moderate Moralism may seem the perfect alternative for these very reasons: not only can it account for these artworks, but it also allows for the idea that the moral character of artworks need not always and necessarily influence the value of art. As we have already seen, this theory claims that moral character only becomes important if it impedes our capacity to engage with the artwork or to respond to it appropriately.

However, and as we already established, the Moderate Moralist runs the risk of offering a theory which on closer scrutiny seems neither properly Moralist nor Autonomist. In addition, it is hard pushed to explain what we are to make of those artworks that are better *qua* art precisely *because* they fail in their moral aim. For although Moderate Moralism allows for the idea that moral virtues and flaws can sometimes also be aesthetic virtues and flaws, it does not seem capable of accepting that a work's moral flaw can sometimes be considered as an aesthetic virtue.

If artworks can be good *in virtue of* (rather than despite) violating our sense of what is morally right, then this is problematic for Ethicism too, for it gives the claim that ethical assessment is relevant to a work's aesthetic merit the wrong valence. As several commentators have argued, a work of art can be valued as art partly on the basis of its morally flawed commitments because such commitments can constitute an integral part of the design and aims of the artwork.[6] To remove a moral flaw under those circumstances would hardly be to make the work better. Rather, it would more likely destroy it, at least in so far as the moral vision presented seems integral to the work as a whole. It seems undeniable that a work that is morally deplorable can be artistically excellent in virtue of having the capacity to present morally deplorable ideas with cogency and conviction.

It is beginning to look, then, as though the issue of morally reprehensible art that is nonetheless good art (perhaps even precisely because of its morally reprehensible character) has a decisive say in this debate that simply cannot be overlooked. For, and as mentioned above in relation to Nabokov's *Lolita*, one of the most fruitful things that a good artwork can do is to get us to assent (albeit temporarily and fictionally) to perspectives that we find morally reprehensible. The distinction that we drew at the very opening of this chapter thus commands our attention again – it seems that the question of whether moral character should influence artistic appraisal actually hangs on whether art must serve a (good) moral purpose to be good as art. In other words, until the matter of immoral yet seemingly aesthetically good art has been settled, we cannot formulate a conclusive answer to the question of whether our moral assessments should influence artistic appraisal or not. Perhaps Jacobson (2005) is right when he argues that there is no true theory of the relation between moral and aesthetic value, and that all one can say is it is possible to formulate a number of true but not necessarily interconnected propositions about that relation as it occurs in particular cases. Putting Jacobson's conclusions aside for the time being, however, it may still be of some use to explore in a little more depth the question of immoral art.

PRELIMINARY CONCLUSIONS:
FROM MORAL VISION TO ARTISTIC VALUE

The philosophical route followed in this chapter has led us from a discussion of art's moral content to its overall worth *qua* art via an at times nearly imperceptible detour into aesthetic character and value. As we saw, Aestheticism, Moralism and Ethicism all endorse a conception of artistic value in which aesthetic value plays an absolutely central role to art's intrinsic value. In fact, at times at least, the distinction between them becomes nearly entirely transparent. Having said that, the two approaches account for the closeness between aesthetic and artistic value in very different ways.

For Aestheticism, the only important kind of value that art can yield is aesthetic value since an artwork's worth is measured exclusively in terms of aesthetically pleasing structure or beautiful form. Aesthetic value is thus equated with artistic value to the extent that aesthetic value is, in fact, the only kind of value capable of determining a work's overall value as art. Surprisingly perhaps, Moralism and Ethicism also define artistic value in roughly aesthetic terms. Aesthetic and artistic value can overlap on this approach because if only theoretically, moral value is cast as distinct from artistic value. That is to say, while moral value certainly is considered a kind of value that can be ascribed to art, strictly speaking, moral value is not constitutive of or to be ranked under artistic value. The question of whether moral content and moral convictions should influence artistic appreciation does, then, target the same concern as whether such content and convictions should have an effect on our aesthetic engagement with it.

However, what the difficult cases we examined towards the end of this chapter show quite clearly is that it is important to distinguish aesthetic appreciation and assessment from artistic appreciation and assessment. For it is only if we keep these two notions apart that we can make sense of cases in which an artwork seems to be both beautiful yet morally flawed, or ugly yet morally praiseworthy. After all, and as we shall see in greater detail in the next chapter, a work can be beautiful yet artistically imperfect or defective because of its moral character. Similarly, an artwork can be ugly yet artistically commendable, again because of its moral character.

CHAPTER 5

MUST ART SERVE A MORAL PURPOSE TO BE GOOD?

IMMORAL ART: CAN ART BE GOOD IN VIRTUE OF ITS IMMORAL CHARACTER?

Paradigmatic examples of highly valued artworks often consist of works that we love and admire in virtue of the unusually delightful and pleasant experience that they give rise to. That is to say, many of the artworks that we consider masterpieces are works that give us a distinctively positive experience, be it simply on account of the pleasure of seeing something particularly elegant or hearing something strikingly beautiful, or the satisfaction of gaining an insight into the workings of our own thoughts or those of others, say. Clearly, these two kinds of features often coincide, and perhaps even feed off each other. Rembrandt's *Portrait of the Artist at his Easel* is thus both a stunning self-portrait and a lens through which we can discern how Rembrandt perceived himself towards the end of his life, and how he understood his experiences to have shaped his outlook on the world. We find the painting rewarding both because of its visual appearance and because of the deeper humanity that he captures in the way he depicts his posture and facial expression.

This commonplace does not imply that *all* the artworks that we deem typical are entirely agreeable to look at, read or listen to. Francis Bacon's *Study of Velasquez's Portrait of Pope Innocent X*, for example, is unpleasant to look at in some respects, but overall yields a very worthwhile and enthralling aesthetic experience. The scene depicted has an element of violence and despair to it, and the colours could be perceived as garish, but the strident yet subtle manner in which Bacon portrays the Pope and his mental state overcomes that initial impression, and we are left with an inspiring and electrifying sense of the work.

Some works push this kind of artistic exploration further still, and cross an ulterior boundary into the less than pleasant with regards to what we find politically, emotionally or morally acceptable. To use an example that we have already discussed, Leni Riefenstahl's film *Triumph of the Will* actively promotes Hitler's moral and political vision, and undoubtedly corrupted the minds of many young Germans during the second half of the 1930s by either instilling or strengthening a thoroughly flawed world-view. What cases such as this film show is that some art may well be said to have a fundamentally detrimental effect on its audience by promoting a view or perspective that is inherently repugnant.

That the morally reprehensible character of such a work is capable of influencing us in more or less undesirable ways is a plain psychological fact. However, the manner in which a morally flawed work can, in virtue of that moral character, have such a powerful effect on our general assessment of the artwork itself may seem more surprising. Interestingly, the relation between the morally reprehensible character of an artwork and that work's aesthetic or artistic value may be said to operate in two directions. First, the moral character of a work such as Riefenstahl's film can be persuasive precisely because it is so beautiful. That is to say, the stunning images, the extraordinary and innovative camera-work, editing and cinematographic design, and the arresting music all contribute to the manipulation of the audience towards a certain political and moral perspective. The work's beauty is so contagious, one may argue, that the ideas and values that they represent seem equally beautiful and worthwhile. Clearly, this is the method traditionally used by most propaganda art in attempting to influence the views of its target audience.

Second, and in a somewhat more complicated fashion, some philosophers have also held the far more contentious claim that it is in fact possible for some artworks to gain an overall positive aesthetic quality *in virtue* of being morally deficient, so that a work's morally reprehensible character may actually constitute an aesthetic or artistic virtue. The Marquis de Sade's literary works are a case in point here. These novels centre around various kinds of very brutal sexual activities that are represented as sexually arousing and spiritually awakening. To the extent that we come to see the cruel and unusual practices in terms of a path to a kind of enlightenment and freedom, then, the depicted brutality solicits responses of excitement in us and not, as one might expect, disgust or horror. Generally speaking, obscene artworks may solicit responses that, even though morally reprehensible, can nonetheless be considered attractive by its audience when expressed or treated in a particular manner, and should therefore, or so it has been held, be regarded as good artworks.[1]

For philosophers defending this 'Immoralist' position, then, a pornographic work can be considered valuable as art precisely in virtue of its obscenity and morally reprehensible character. On this account, our experience of some works, such as those by the Marquis de Sade, is actively enhanced by the morally flawed attitude commended to us. What matters, in other words, is not so much whether or not the moral perspective endorsed is one we take to be merited in reality, but, rather, whether it is conveyed in such a way that we find intelligible or plausible, or otherwise that the psychological experience of participating in the imaginary world in question is understood to be worthwhile in virtue of, or participatory in, a coherent object of art.

The question of whether, as Immoralists claim, there really can be artworks that are good artworks at least partly because of their flawed moral character obviously has a vital bearing on the issues discussed in the two previous chapters. For if Immoralism is correct, it has serious philosophical consequences for both Autonomism and Aestheticism on the one hand, and Moralism and Ethicism on the other, and may play a determining role in the process of settling whether we should let our moral convictions influence our overall assessments of artworks or not.

To dismiss Autonomism and Aestheticism as significant contenders in the debate that has driven much of Part II could be seen as a quick task if the Immoralist's idea is to be accepted, since even the 'Sophisticated' version of Aestheticism can't allow for direct (positive) influence between moral and aesthetic value. For it nearly goes without saying that to hold a philosophical position whereby an artwork's moral character may occasionally influence its overall value albeit only (i) indirectly, and (ii) if that moral character mars or promotes the work's aesthetically valuable features (where it is assumed that a negative moral character may only mar the overall value of the artwork), is not compatible with the claim that art can be valuable as art precisely *in virtue* of having a morally reprehensible character.

Similarly, if an artwork could be valuable in virtue of its immoral character, then this seems to constitute a strong argument against Ethicism and Moderate Moralism, for, as we saw in Chapter 4, these theories rely on the idea that, to the extent to which we deem the responses solicited from us by an artwork to be morally prohibited, we will either fail to respond in that way or deem the response to be unmerited.[2] There seems to be no room, in other words, for the Immoralist claim within a Moralist or Ethicist framework either. However, and as we shall soon see in greater detail, it is the latter approach that may well stand a better chance of accommodating the Immoralist intuition, since it, contrary to Autonomism or Aestheticism, at least allows for the possibility that there can be a direct influence between moral character and overall artistic value. That is to say, the framework, if not the particular route prescribed, seems friendly to the Immoralist possibility.

In order to proceed with our enquiry, then, it will be necessary to establish whether the Immoralist claim is credible and well-grounded. According to Matthew Kieran, there are three good reasons to think that it is sound and adequately founded (2003b: 460–1). First, obscene art can appeal to some of our morally prohibited desires – desires that one might find arousing in art but that one would not gain pleasure from in reality. One may find, say, that the Marquis de Sade's works solicit some of our desires in virtue of representing some sexual fantasies that we find arousing *qua* fantasies, but would not necessarily find equally exciting were we to enact or be subjected to them ourselves in real life. Second, obscene art may fulfil our 'meta-desire', for example, to break free from certain psychological or moral taboos: we may thus find delight in the idea of being someone who lacks some of the inhibitions that we actually do have. Third, some representation may be obscene in virtue of representing something in a morally reprehensible way, and yet solicit our attention and favourable response by appealing to some cognitive interests of ours (such as photographs of deformed bodies). The idea here, Kieran emphasizes, is not that we take pleasure in the represented person's pain or disfigurement but, rather, that our curiosity and fascination (in this case with deformed bodies) are satisfied by the representation (of deformed bodies).

Armed with these three kinds of reasons, let us consider the Immoralist proposition in the light of three examples. To illustrate the first kind of case that may be cited in support of Immoralism, William Burroughs' *Junkie: Confessions of an Unredeemed Drug*

Addict presents us with the perspective of an unapologetic heroin addict for whom the spiritual freedoms brought by drugs override any negative aspects that a life of injection, petty theft and squalor involves. The main character is unashamedly selfish and defiant in the pursuit of satisfying his own addiction, and the pleasure and insight he gains from leading a junkie's life is represented as being a fair exchange to any inconvenience or unhappiness it may cause to others.

Whilst the moral perspective imposed upon the readers of this novel is indisputably morally reprehensible, the response it aims to solicit from us is one of feeling liberated and uninhibited: it aims to question our attitudes to and belief in society's moral norms by enabling us to identify with the main character and his vision. That is to say, as our reading progresses, we begin to grasp the freedom implicit in what is presented as an entirely legitimate ambition, namely to allow oneself to be absolutely self-serving. We may even experience a sense of unreserved and spontaneous freedom ourselves, simply through the experience of finding our own attitudes tested and undermined and perhaps – although this is not necessarily part of the work – even reaffirmed. The style chosen by Burroughs to convey this perspective and lifestyle is then also best described as particularly immediate: we are immersed into a thought-process that is self-obsessed and which never deviates from its sole ambition by a narrative that is similarly direct and egotistical. In this way, Burroughs manages to create a fictional world in which we can quite easily find the narrator's anti-social existence enviable, as the work solicits one's desire to abandon oneself completely to our most self-indulgent, and even self-destructive, urges.

For the great majority of Burroughs' readers, however, this is a pleasure to be gained through fictional worlds alone: a reader who responds in the manner solicited by the novel is likely not to gain such a sense of freedom and inhibition were she really a junkie herself. But what this novel achieves is to present us with the perspective of a heroin addict in a remarkably realistic and interesting way. This, in turn, enables us to have the fictional experience from which we gain a certain enjoyment and insight. At least in this respect, then, it seems that some works can be good artworks precisely because they promote a view and perspective that is morally reprehensible.

The second kind of reason given by Kieran shows that immoral art may allegedly fulfil some of our 'meta-desires'. A case in point here may be Maurizio Cattelan's *The Ninth Hour*. This work represents a statue of Pope John Paul II struck down by a meteor. The Pope is surrounded by broken glass, and although he is clearly in severe pain (the meteor is still covering his legs), he is still holding on to a big brass cross. The floor is covered by a thick red carpet, and the overall impression given by the work is that one has just witnessed some horrible accident in which the Pope has been fatally wounded.

The symbolism of this work speaks for itself – the Head of the Catholic Church, for many God's personification on Earth, is portrayed as vulnerable, pathetic and undesirable. All that which the Catholic faith holds as sacred and true is represented as feeble and moribund. The expressive language used by Cattelan is shocking to most, and terribly offensive in particular to Catholics and most believers of any religious faith. However, to someone who is not particularly sympathetic to Catholicism or religion as such, it may well arouse not only shock, but also a sense of pleasure in virtue of breaking this both moral and political taboo. That is to say, to someone who would never actually want the Pope or any religious leader to be humiliated and killed in such a horrible way in reality, and perhaps not even fictionally, this work may nonetheless be deemed good *qua* art precisely because of the shocking point it makes and the manner in which it may encourage one to experience this artwork as if one were someone with no moral restraints or taboos. Cattelan's means of representation are very effective, and we may thereby be enticed into feeling that we are indulging in some utterly unacceptable perspective. We are, in other words, enjoying the fact that the morally reprehensible vision this work offers is one in which we take some pleasure because of the very wickedness of that perspective. In other words, we find delight in the idea of being someone who lacks some of the inhibitions that we in reality do have.

The third reason that may lend plausibility to Immoralism can be illustrated by The Chapman Brothers' *Hell*. This work consists of eight model landscapes very explicitly and elaborately representing a great variety of torture and physical pain. With remarkable detail and precision, the Chapman Brothers have cast, painted and positioned over five thousand miniature persons, most of which are either naked or clad in Nazi uniforms. Every miniature is enforcing or undergoing hideous acts of torture.

Without exception, the horror of the scenes depicted is harrowing and, moreover, intensified by the impressive scale of the work (in total the work covers 28 square feet). But the remarkable sense of detail and precision may nonetheless fascinate us. It is precisely because every feature of this work has been so carefully designed and executed that our interest may be grabbed by the work, and we may not only be tempted to examine every facet of these hellish scenarios, but also gain some satisfaction from it. As Kieran is prudent to point out, it is not that we gain pleasure from the suffering of the miniatures. Rather, it is an interest in the inflicted suffering that, when satisfied, gives us a certain kind of pleasurable experience. Thus, in defence of Immoralism, it does seem possible for a work like *Hell* to solicit our attention and favourable response by appealing to some interest (such as morbid fascination) which, when fulfilled, yields a certain kind of cognitive gratification.

All in all, then, the Immoralist claim does seem to have significant bite when it comes to examples of artworks that do not fit easily within our normal moral norms. The suggestion it advances is not that most artistic appreciation operates in this fashion, or even that much of it does. All it needs to maintain in order to have some philosophical clout is that *some* artworks are good *qua* art in virtue of their being morally flawed, or of presenting a morally reprehensible view. What the three kinds of cases outlined above have shown is that there seem to be several ways in which this claim may be held as true. The psychology of artistic appreciation and assessment can, in other words, allow for even greater complexity than the straightforward Immoralist intuition that we started off by examining.

If room must be made within the framework of philosophical theory for Immoralism, does that imply that both approaches explored in the previous chapter are to be rejected outright? After all, some of the tenets at the very heart of those approaches seem anathema to the possibility of art that is good because of its morally flawed character.

Whilst it seems impossible to revise Sophisticated Aesthetic or Ethicism to incorporate the Immoralist claim for reasons outlined above, it has been argued that Moderate Moralism can be reformulated in order to allow for the genuine artistic value and appreciation of works such as *Hell*, *The Ninth Hour* and *Junkie*. On this revised version, dubbed 'Most Moderate Moralism' (Kieran 2001a), the moral features implicit in and central to the imaginative experience afforded by an artwork are relevant to an artwork's intrinsic value, but only to the extent that those features mar or promote the intelligibility of the characters, events, situations and responses as represented. Emphasis is thus placed on the kind of imaginative experience that immoral works can invite us to engage in, and this positive experience can, in turn, yield roughly the same structure of influence that the work itself can yield on the more traditional version of Moderate Moralism. It may, then, be possible to respond to an artwork created a long time ago in the manner solicited by that work even though it may have moral features that one may find morally reprehensible, such as finding some acts of chivalry romantic even though they imply a diminished view of women's abilities and rights.

Most Moderate Moralism is thus a theory that sets out to remain Moralist by nature with the added capacity to incorporate the Immoralist claim. It does so by placing more philosophical weight on the imaginative experience that a work invites us to engage in, and by focusing on the element of intelligibility. However, it remains questionable (at best) whether this view can rightly be described as Moralist. For not only does it allow for the idea that a work's value may be increased as art partly in virtue of its moral character (which is in line with Moralism), it accepts that the work's immoral character may be an aesthetic virtue. And this seems at least to be quite straightforwardly at odds with Moralism's basic tenet.

Regardless of whether one is willing to commit to Most Moderate Moralism, then, it seems likely that Immoralism does render the two kinds of theory discussed in the previous chapter problematic. That is to say, neither seems capable of providing us with a comprehensive and plausible account of how we are to formalize the relation between a work's moral character and its overall value as art. Perhaps adequate theories can be given by these approaches for artworks that fit the paradigmatic model of an artwork that this chapter began by sketching. But if a unitary thesis of *all* artworks is what is sought, then the Immoralist claim certainly seems to have done considerable damage to both the Moralist and Autonomist projects.

A RETURN TO COGNITIVISM VIA IMAGINATION

A particularly interesting aspect of the suggestion discussed above concerns the role that is ascribed to the imagination in artistic appreciation and the way in which it is brought to the fore of philosophical discussion. As we have seen, the imaginative experience highlighted by Most Moderate Moralism is one which claims to lead to a better understanding of the work's subject and treatment of it. For example, by engaging imaginatively with *Beowulf* we can not only come to respond as solicited to the acts of alleged heroism of the main protagonist (even though we in reality might find his actions reprehensible), we can perhaps also come to better understand the saga and the lessons to be drawn from it. This idea seems to highlight one of Immoralism's most promising features, namely how engaging with a morally flawed work may yield understanding and knowledge into a certain perspective.

For supporters of Immoralism can hold that artworks with pornographic or excessively violent content may be valuable at least partly because they enable us to increase our understanding of moral views that we do not personally endorse.[3] This view, better known as 'Cognitive Immoralism', thus upholds the Immoralist claim together with a point about the cognitive value that immoral art may yield: the main idea is that a work's value as art can be enhanced in virtue of its immoral character because imaginatively experiencing morally flawed or reprehensible responses in ways that are morally problematic can deepen one's understanding and appreciation of art and the subject of which it treats.

Immoral art, or the examination of the very possibility of art that is good in virtue of its morally reprehensible character, has thus led us back to the question of Cognitivism. Could it be, then, that the legitimacy of Immoralism somehow depends on whether it can yield a form of knowledge or not?

Cognitive Immoralism emphasizes the claim that morally flawed art can give us knowledge of certain concepts, situations or character traits in experiential terms. For the theory rests on the idea that having a certain kind of experience, even by proxy as in the case of art, is a particularly important way of coming to know what that kind of experience in general is like.[4] What is more, Cognitive Immoralism assumes that the appreciation and understanding of the nature of an experience admits of degrees and depends on our ability to endorse different perspectives on important elements of our experience. Most importantly, however, Cognitive Immoralists hold that experiencing morally flawed responses may afford a kind of comparative experience or perspective that could not otherwise be had. The Cognitive Immoralist may even argue that one has a duty to seek out morally flawed experiences and experience things in morally reprehensible ways in cases where one lacks a full and proper understanding of morally commendable experiences of the relevant kind.

Central to Cognitive Immoralism is thus the idea that it is possible to suspend our personal moral judgements or, further still, to take up moral judgements and responses in imagination that we would not endorse in reality. However, this point has been contested in at least two ways. In the first instance, it has been argued by Tamar Gendler that we may not actually *want* to engage with fictional scenarios that are radically opposed to our own moral convictions. For Gendler, this unwillingness to imagine morally deviant situations can be traced back to 'a general desire not to be manipulated into taking on points of views that we would not reflectively endorse as authentically our own' and is to be explained in terms of imagination involving something between belief and 'mere supposition' (2000: 56).

In the second instance, Kendall Walton (1994) has held that even if we were to want to engage with morally flawed perspectives in the way recommended by immoral art, we are actually *incapable* of meaningfully engaging with fiction that we find morally reprehensible. It is impossible to imaginatively engage with, for example, the perspective promoted by Leni Riefenstahl in her *Triumph of the Will* in a way such that we can legitimately say that we have acquired some form of understanding and knowledge of the concepts involved. Whilst it may be possible to gain some sympathy, say, for the citizens of the Third Reich that were mesmerized by this stunning film and, as a result, endorsed the Nazi vision themselves, we cannot say that we have acquired any further understanding for that perspective in any significant sense.

To this complaint, Cognitive Immoralists reply that what matters in relation to the appreciation and assessment of art is whether the moral perspective a work conveys is rendered intelligible or psychologically credible, and not whether the moral perspective of a work is what we take to be the right one. Rather, what is important is if the artist can get us to see, feel and respond to the world as represented as she intends us to and how, in so doing, we come to more fully understand and appreciate things we might not otherwise have done. All we have to do is to take up some form of conditional assent to the states of affairs represented, and do so only within the boundaries imposed by the work's status as art.[5]

The concern is a difficult one to resolve, because although the points raised by Gendler and Walton are important, we have already granted the main Immoralist claim, namely that some works of art do seem to have artistic value precisely in virtue of advocating a morally reprehensible perspective. Perhaps, then, the difficulty is one more directly targeted at the Cognitivist addition: should the claim to knowledge through imaginative experience be abandoned in order to save Immoralism as such? However, if we answer this question affirmatively, we will, in a first instance, have an argument against Most Moderate Moralism that is independent of whether it can truly be considered a version of Moralism or not. More importantly, however, we will reject the account that seemed to have the resources to add legitimacy to Immoralism as a philosophical theory in its own right alongside Moralism and Autonomism.

Unfortunately, however, rejecting Cognitive Immoralism is precisely what we must do, because on a closer scrutiny it becomes clear that the account has aspirations and goals that it simply cannot attain. The insights that we may, on occasion, be able to gain from engaging imaginatively with morally flawed works do not qualify as moral knowledge *per se* because there is a limit to the extent that we can hold our imaginative engagement with Riefenstahl's world-view to give us genuine understanding and knowledge of that perspective. Engaging imaginatively with the film may lead us to acquire a deeper insight into what it must have been like to idolize Hitler, or to feel exalted by Nazi ideals, but whether it is because we just don't want (Gendler) or because we cannot (Walton) take on that perspective fully, this psychological *rapprochement* cannot be said to yield moral knowledge that can unreservedly be considered substantial.

What is more, and as Carroll (2000) has argued, even though Cognitivist Immoralism may provide us with a good argument against the censorship of immoral art, the account affords an overly instrumentalist justification of such art. Art should not be vindicated purely in terms of the knowledge it may give us even if it is capable of yielding knowledge. Whilst it may be considered an advantage for art that it can help us get a better grasp of certain difficult notions or thought-processes, we must be careful not to reduce art to an epistemological tool. The reasons why we value art are, as we established in Chapter 2, numerous, and that diversity is something every account of art must be able to make room for if it is to be taken seriously.

THE LIMITS OF MORAL PURPOSE AND THE QUESTION OF CENSORSHIP

The question of whether art should ever be censored, and if so when, is surely one of the areas in which philosophical investigations into art have the most extensive ramifications into our everyday life. For art, in virtue of both its aesthetic, moral and cognitive value, can have the power to corrupt our moral vision or legitimize morally reprehensible behaviour. However, it is now clear that there is an important distinction to be drawn between the claim that art *can* have a negative moral effect at times, and the idea that there is something intrinsic to art with a morally reprehensible character that *necessarily* leads it to have a negative effect on its audience. That is to say, there is a difference between admitting that a work such as Burrough's *Junkie* may have encouraged someone to adopt the life and priorities of a drug addict, and holding that all art with morally flawed content automatically has a detrimental effect on us.[6]

This distinction is particularly noteworthy in relation to the question of censorship. For if art with immoral content, contra the stronger of these two claims, should not always be censored, when, if at all, should it? Underlying one of the most convincing reasons for holding that art should at least at times be censored is Arthur Danto's concern about the way in which art that is morally flawed can prevent or block us from acting appropriately in certain circumstances.[7] According to Danto, 'there is something wrong in writing plays about that sort of injustice in which we have an obligation to intervene, since it puts the audience at just the sort of distance' (1981: 22) that may hinder them from acting appropriately in a particular circumstance. The idea here is that when we engage with artworks, we take up a stance that in itself acts as a kind of barrier and which prevents us from acting or responding in the manner that the situation calls for. Extrapolating from Danto's claim, then, one might hold that immoral art that hinders us from acting appropriately should thus be censored. Here, one may say, lies the limit to how good immoral art can be.

The 'distance' that Danto refers to is the 'psychical' one that we are already familiar with from Chapter 4, namely the attitude we should or tend to assume in aesthetic appreciation.[8] But as we noted in the previous chapter, Edward Bullough's 'psychical distance' is an important tool for supporters of Autonomism, and now we see that the philosophical approach that is Aestheticism has some very practical consequences. For if we are to hold that the qualities that we assess in artistic appreciation are only the artwork's formal qualities, it seems that censoring – let alone condoning – a work for its immoral character is not really available to us. If Aestheticism is true, there can be no sound philosophical argument for artistic censorship. So, Danto's point only applies to immoral art as understood by theories that require artistic appreciation to involve some kind of psychological distance from the moral content of the work, and thereby reveals that Aestheticism may not have the resources to censor art (for one cannot ground censorship simply on the claim that some immoral content mars the aesthetic value of the work alone).

Interestingly, and as Mary Devereaux has pointed out in a somewhat Immoralist spirit, the reason why the Aestheticist strategy fails with regards to works such as *Triumph of the Will* is that distancing ourselves from the morally objectionable elements of the film means distancing ourselves from those features of the film that make it the work of art that it is (1998: 243). That is to say, if we simply overlook the moral content of the work and focus entirely on its strictly formal qualities, we do not do the work justice because we fail to enter into it, so to speak. To express the matter bluntly, to fail to engage with the moral issues raised by such a film is to fail to engage with the film itself.

Now, none of this is to say that we must endorse Cognitive Immoralism and thereby be confronted with the difficulties about imaginative resistance formulated by Gendler and Walton and no doubt other problems too. The claim here is merely that if, in our artistic appreciation of *Triumph of the Will*, we disregard the fact that it is a documentary film intended as propaganda for Hitler's National-Socialist party we are, in a significant sense, engaging with a completely different artwork. The moral vision promoted by the work is such an important part of its overall character that it cannot be ignored. Importantly, too, this remains the case whether one sees the film from a sympathetic standpoint, as many of its early viewers did, or from an opposed one, as most viewers are likely to do today. Indeed, it seems likely that the film is a great deal more interesting as an artwork from a liberal perspective (and the disgust at Nazism implied by that perspective), for the simple reason that our resistance to the message propagated by the film makes us more aware of the film's construction and artistry.

It is not obvious, then, that there can ever be a philosophically viable and principled reason for censoring art. This is not to say, of course, that so doing would not at times bring about some advantages from a strictly psychological or sociological point of view. Practically speaking, in other words, we may well have excellent reasons to prohibit the exposure of some artworks. Propaganda art can, after all, be very powerful and corrupt minds in a way that mere facts might not, and so art can undeniably have very negative effects. However, even though it might be beneficial for one person or even society at large to disallow certain art, the case of immoral art reveals the difficulty, if not impossibility, of developing a standardized rule on this matter. Art is a means of expression – be it of emotions, political ideals or moral belief systems – and not a means of coercion. As such there is no reason to censor it any more than we do speech.

CONCLUSIONS

The question of whether art can have moral value has taken three forms in Part II. First, in Chapter 3 we asked whether art can yield moral knowledge and, if so, how wide-ranging and significant that knowledge may be with regards to the value of art in general. In this context, we concluded that art is indeed capable of giving us moral knowledge and that the doctrine of Cognitivism is to be endorsed in the case of art. Most importantly perhaps, we established that art's ability to yield moral understanding is a feature closely connected to its intrinsic value. Since, however, aesthetic value can also be cast in that role, there certainly are avenues in which mutual influence can be exercised between aesthetic and moral value. Further exploration of this possible interaction at the level of art appreciation was thus called for.

Second, and following up on the lesson gained from the previous chapter, in Chapter 4 we examined whether our moral convictions, both those previously held and those originating in a work's moral content, should be allowed to influence our overall appreciation and assessment of art. What we learnt from examining the two main opposing approaches to this problem was that neither Aestheticism on the one hand, nor Moralism and Ethicism on the other hand, can incorporate some very important aspects of artistic assessment. That is to say, what the problematic cases we looked at in some detail indicate is that the accounts offered by these theories are simply too narrow: if we cannot accommodate for works that are less traditional from an appreciative point of view, we will be left with philosophical theories that are, at best, only applicable to one kind of artwork. The consequence of such an undesirable outcome is, obviously, that no unitary account of art can be given. What needs to be developed in this area of philosophical investigation, then, is a new framework that overcomes the limitations of the debate and provides us with a fresh spectrum of philosophical alternatives.

Third, we addressed the case of immoral art directly or, more specifically, artworks that seem good in virtue of having a morally reprehensible character. In Chapter 5 we thus examined whether it is possible for some artworks to have artistic value precisely because of promoting a morally flawed world-view or understanding of a particular person or event. Moreover, we posed the question of whether art, to be good, ought to have a moral purpose. In the first instance, we established that whilst some artworks can be said to be good *despite* their flawed moral character, others are good *in virtue* of their morally reprehensible vision. For appreciating the artistic or aesthetic qualities with which a certain perspective or vision is portrayed is not the same as finding that vision morally attractive; we may find a work beautiful, say, whilst considering its content deeply revolting. In a second instance, and although we concluded that art need not serve a moral purpose to be good *qua* art, we suggested that any ambitions to build up a good philosophical argument for censoring art seems unlikely to succeed.

PART III

BEAUTY AND MORAL GOODNESS

CHAPTER 6

KANT'S THEORY OF BEAUTY, MORALITY AND FREEDOM

CONCEPTUAL DEPENDENCE AND LOGICAL PRIORITY

We now know that the relation between Aesthetics and Morality operates at more than one level: not only can it be difficult to separate the aesthetic realm from the moral one *qua* field of philosophical investigation, as we saw in Part I, but it can also be hard to distinguish the sphere of influence of aesthetic value from that of moral value with regards to particular artworks, as we discussed in Part II. The question we started off by exploring is thus seen to have changed shape in accordance with our particular focus of examination. With every new area of enquiry, that is to say, the account to be given of the relation between the aesthetic and the moral alters in both content and style, ranging from issues concerning the limits of aesthetic experience to questions about the overall worth of art the moral content of which is reprehensible. In the midst of all this variation, complexity and seeming confusion, then, it seems certain that the best way to understand the relation between the aesthetic and the moral is, first and foremost, in terms of a *set* of associations. In other words, there is not really such a thing as *the* question of how to account for the connection between Aesthetics and Morality but, rather, a whole host of queries and concerns.

One suggestion that we touched upon briefly in Chapter 1 and that we must now turn to consider in greater detail is the idea, encapsulated by several different theories in various different ways, that aesthetic and moral value are to a certain extent inseparable in so far as the paradigmatic instances of such value – beauty and moral goodness – are more or less ontologically equivalent. The relation between Aesthetics and Morality is thus conceived in terms of the close alliance that quite naturally prevails between two notions that are not only closely linked but, in actual fact, overlapping to a considerable degree.

Heralding the idea at the heart of this suggestion, Plato is generally understood to hold that beauty and goodness are closely related on a metaphysical level. In the *Phaedrus*, for example, Plato discusses beauty in terms of that which awakens our desire for the morally good: our perception of beauty is part of what motivates us towards virtue and knowledge of the good (2005: esp. §254b). Similarly, in the *Philebus*, beauty is held to be at the very root of the good life. More explicitly, in the *Symposium*, beauty is said to be the object of our highest – and so inevitably moral – aspirations: the search for beauty necessarily lies along the philosopher's path towards knowledge of the good in itself. In a similar vein, Aquinas writes in his neo-Platonic *Summa Theologiae* that 'beauty and goodness in a thing are identical fundamentally, for they are based upon the same thing, namely, the form' (1997: 47). What is more, for Aquinas the two notions share a goal: the morally good leads us to achieve our ideal ends, and beauty leads us to contemplate the achievement of that fulfilment.

Although seemingly far removed from Platonic metaphysics, many eighteenth-century investigations into the two notions share this perspective of overlapping kinds of value. Shaftesbury argues, for instance, that 'beauty and good are still the same' in so far as the two notions are constituted by the same property, namely harmony (2004: 327). Accordingly, and as we shall see in greater detail in Chapter 7, Shaftesbury understands our perception of the beautiful as being of precisely the same order as our knowledge and experience of the good: both our aesthetic and moral sensitivities are directed towards the harmonious ordering of the universe. In both cases, then, the sentiment associated with beauty or moral goodness is attuned to the healthy functioning of our natural environment which exists, as it were, for our good.

This idea that the sense of both beauty and moral goodness consists in an awareness of the natural law or order is present, in various ways, throughout the eighteenth century, occurring in various versions in Hutcheson, Rousseau, and, as we shall see in greater detail, in Hume and Kant as well. Explicitly, too, in his attempt to revise and clarify what he considered to be the central element of Immanuel Kant's *Critique of the Power of Judgement*, the poet and philosopher Friedrich Schiller argues that our sense of beauty works toward specifically moral ends. To this end, Schiller holds that what he calls aesthetic education – the immersion of the subject in a profound and thoughtful relation to objects of beauty – has a specifically moral end. That is to say, in contradistinction to many of his contemporaries for whom the problem of taste was a specifically artistic and cultural issue, Schiller held that a deep acquaintance with the fine arts should play an essential part in man's effort to attune himself to a desire for the common good. The cultivation of taste, in other words, is a necessary part of our moral education.

Clearly, then, theories that uphold that beauty and goodness are one and the same ontologically speaking are particularly interesting for our purposes, especially so in light of how they conceive the connection between the broader notions of Aesthetics and Morality. For in one sense, there is no novel and substantial account to be given of that relation if beauty and moral goodness are so close as to imply one another. If, in other words, beauty and goodness in a thing are, in Aquinas' words, 'identical fundamentally', what we are investigating is not so much an association between two separate notions as an account of how it is that they are two instances of the same thing. From this perspective, then, the conceptual dependence of the aesthetic and the moral is grounded in a way which other accounts that also allow for some such dependence cannot grant: if beauty and goodness are ontologically equivalent, the conceptual dependence between aesthetic and moral value is not just a practical matter brought out by our assessments of particular objects of aesthetic appreciation – and our awareness of some, possibly unrelated, cases of the interdependence of aesthetic and moral value – but, rather, a metaphysical question overarching any individual manifestations of such value. Indeed, the claim from Wittgenstein with which we began our enquiry in Chapter 1, although it must initially have appeared – and was evidently intended to appear – counter-intuitive, now seems to have much deeper and more philosophically continuous roots than was at first suspected. The idea that 'Ethics and Aesthetics are one and the same' (1961: §6.421), while it still raises significant problems, can at least now be seen to reflect a tradition of thought observant of the two realms' fundamental similarity.

In reflecting on these theories it is also important to note that there is nothing to suggest that beauty and goodness cannot remain conceptually distinct even though they may ultimately necessarily be accounted for in terms of one another, at least in onto-logical and metaphysical terms. The idea that beauty and goodness cannot be separated at the most fundamental plane does not, in other words, automatically disprove the results established towards the end of Part II, namely that beauty and goodness *can* come apart at the level of appreciation in particular artworks. After all, particular moral assessments vary from epoch to epoch and society to society in a way similar to that of aesthetic taste, regardless of whether it may be possible to observe underlying truths. It may also be argued that the very fact that the moral and aesthetic do *not* necessarily intersect is in itself a moral reflection on the culture and society in which this is the case. That is to say, the very fact that what we find beautiful does not always appear to be also an instance of goodness may have as much to do with the disalignment of our individual and communal sensibilities as it has anything fundamental to do with the nature of the beautiful and the good. Indeed, this sense in which education of aesthetic sensibility is to be understood in terms of a realignment of our sense of the good and beautiful seems highly germane to the concerns of many of the accounts we have mentioned, from Plato through to Rousseau and Schiller.

In individual cases, then, although one might want to say that there is much about a film such as Riefenstahl's *Triumph of the Will* that is beautiful in spite of its clear portrayal of a morally corrupt world-view – and thus observe the separation of beauty and goodness in this particular instance – one may still resist describing the film as beautiful *tout court* or be unwilling to ascribe the highest form of aesthetic praise to it. This reluctance to overlook the morally flawed character of the work even when we engage with it aesthetically could, then, be explained in virtue of this fundamental coincidence between beauty and goodness. On this view, the reason why we cannot perhaps claim that *Triumph of the Will* is absolutely beautiful without qualification may precisely consist in this overlap of moral and aesthetic value at the deepest level of philosophical enquiry.[1] It seems, then, that the hard cases discussed in Chapter 4 may not necessarily rule out this approach to Aesthetics and Morality. In fact, and as we have just seen, it could even be said to explain the duality of such difficult cases.

Having said that, some of the concerns raised in Chapter 5 about art that seems to gain in aesthetic merit because of their morally suspect or unsavoury content cannot quite so easily be accounted for on this approach. While it is one thing to say that morally flawed works can – albeit often in a relatively superficial sense – still be beautiful, it is an altogether different claim to hold that a work is beautiful *in virtue* of its morally flawed character. That is to say, if we are set on upholding the Platonic equivalence claim, we cannot accept the Immoralist claim, at least not at face value. However, for reasons already outlined and discussed in Chapter 5, this claim is important and must be incorporated into the relation between aesthetic and moral value, for there are works, such as William Burroughs' *Junkie*, that do acquire their aesthetic and artistic value precisely because of the morally reprehensible perspective they exemplify. And this, quite clearly, must certainly prove something of a stumbling block for any approach based on the idea that beauty and goodness are fundamentally one and the same.

At this stage in our enquiry, two things should be apparent. First, the Wittgensteinian claim with which we began – to the effect that 'Aesthetics and Ethics are one and the same' – can be applied in both a weak sense and a strong sense. If we are to pursue the strong sense, which we have just been discussing, then we are bound to the view that, on a metaphysical and ontological level, the paradigmatic instances of ethical and aesthetic value coincide; and that, where they appear not to coincide, the problem lies with our individual sensibility or wider culture. If we limit ourselves to the weaker version of the claim, however, we are bound only to observe the significant interplay between aesthetic and ethical value, and draw conclusions as seem appropriate to particular cases. Here, then, the question arises as to which of the routes we should pursue. Furthermore, if some version of the stronger claim is to be defended, should the metaphysical and ontological overlap be taken to suggest an identity relation, or something more akin to a symbolic relation? As we shall see in greater detail, it is this latter construal that is preferred by Kant, who argues that beauty is a formal symbol of the good.

Second, we must bear in mind that the stronger version of the claim is deeply troubled by the cases appealed to by the Immoralist approach, namely that some things are beautiful *in virtue of* their immoral content. The suggestion that the relation between Aesthetics and Morality is to be understood in terms of two instances of one and the same thing is unlikely to succeed if we give it a strict and narrow reading. Aesthetically good yet morally flawed art shows that comprehensive ontological (and conceptual) equivalence may be too strong an account of the relation under scrutiny here.

Nevertheless, it is important to note that the rejection of a metaphysical identity between the beautiful and the good does not rule out there still being some kind of logical priority between the two notions, and by extension between the aesthetic and moral domains in general. On the contrary, it is only if a strict philosophical equivalence is held to obtain between them that it makes sense to hold that goodness should not be conceived as somehow derivative of beauty or vice versa. On a weaker reading, some kind of logical dependency may well be seen to prevail. The question remains, however, as to which should be held to be logically prior. Is the notion of beauty to be derived from that of the good, or vice versa?

As Marcia Muelder Eaton (1997) has pointed out, however, few philosophers have defended the view that goodness is derivative of beauty. For in the light of Morality's extensive normative scope, it seems improbable that our moral life could find its source ultimately in something quite so difficult to pin down as the idea of beauty. Very often a course of action that seems morally right will be distinguished by its indifference to aesthetic matters. If, for example, it is held to be our duty to replace all the old tungsten lightbulbs in our house with lightbulbs of the energy-saving, fluorescent variety, the fact that we may happen to find fluorescent light cold and unpleasant does not enter into the equation, so to speak, or at least not in the moral equation. Similarly, an employer who decided that only beautiful and young people should be given jobs would clearly be in breach of her or his duty to abide by the norms of equal opportunity, whether this is backed up by legislation or not. Indeed, in a Socratean vein, it is very often held to be the case that those people or things that appear to be beautiful are the most morally suspect.[2] To come to find the famously dishevelled Socrates beautiful, in spite of his tangled beard, unkempt clothing and snub nose, would be to come to appreciate his intellectual and moral qualities.

If we pursue this common if somewhat clichéd view, however, we find that the appeal to the vanity of external beauty usually works by referring to the 'inner beauty' of something. That is to say, in taking no trouble over his appearance (except, possibly, the trouble to appear as dishevelled as possible), we could argue that Socrates was in a sense simply trying to defer our judgement about his beauty or not by asking us to consider his person and mind rather than his clothes, beard and bare feet. And where we refer, in such cases, to the 'inner beauty' of persons, as often as not we will be pointing to moral qualities. Could there be another, less conversational sense, then, in which the notion of moral goodness is logically underwritten by the idea of beauty? This question we must leave open for the time being.

KANT'S ACCOUNT OF BEAUTY AS THE SYMBOL OF MORALITY

Kant's texts are notoriously dense, but even a brief study of the main claims made in his *Critique of the Power of Judgement* will tell us that what is being presented is not an isolated aesthetic theory. Rather, Kant's account of aesthetic judgement is clearly presented in the light of its forming a part – and a crucial part at that – of an entire philosophical system. That is to say, for Kant, to philosophize about beauty is also to reflect on our wider epistemology, philosophy of mind, metaphysics and moral theory. Beauty is thus inherently tied in with the notions most central to human life in general: the possibility of acquiring knowledge and making generally valid assertions; the mental abilities exercised in both our intellectual and affective encounters with the world and its contents; the underlying and constitutive principles of systematicity and regularity in nature as well as thought; and the pursuit of virtuous character and other moral aspirations.

In Section 59 of the third *Critique* Kant famously states the point that much of his previous discussion has been leading up to, namely that beauty is the symbol of morality. In general, the relation between the aesthetic and the moral takes two main expressions for Kant: one is focused on moral feeling and the way in which beauty can attune us to such feeling; the other is concerned with moral and aesthetic judgement and the so-called 'autonomy' thereof. Without suggesting that these are two completely distinct ways of approaching Kant's claim, it is possible to discuss them in relative isolation from one another. So, let us take a brief look at these main strands in order to establish whether there is indeed a sense in which beauty can rightly be described as the symbol of morality in the manner Kant indicates.

First, a propensity to take an interest in beauty (especially the beauty of nature) is said to be suggestive of 'a good soul' and a 'mental attunement favorable to moral feeling' (Kant 2000: §42; 298–9). Experiencing beauty thus serves as a 'propaedeutic' or preparation for morality, in so far as it encourages the 'development of moral ideas and the culture of moral feeling' (2000: §60; 356). The beautiful, Kant states, 'prepares us to love something, even nature, without interest' (2000: §29; 266–7). That is to say, the admiration of beauty teaches us to love things for themselves, or without referring to what they can do for us. This idea that things *in themselves* are the objects of our moral and aesthetic perceptions is crucial to Kant's approach.

Second, beauty serves as the symbol of morality in that an aesthetic judgement 'legislates for itself' and is not 'subjected to a heteronomy of laws of experience' (2000: §59; 353). That is to say, judgements about beauty are not governed by rules; they are not the result of inferential reasoning. Instead, they are always based on the subject's individual experience of a certain kind of pleasure.

The idea that judgements about beauty must always be based on the subject's own feeling of pleasure does not necessarily restrain its epistemological reach: for Kant, aesthetic judgements demand universal assent (2000: §59). An aesthetic judgement is thus not merely one individual subject's report of her purely idiosyncratic experience of a thing's aesthetic character. Instead, such a judgement reflects how subjects in general respond aesthetically to a certain object, for an aesthetic judgement's claim to universal agreement is grounded in the idea that we all have the same mental abilities and that those abilities operate in very similar ways in comparable circumstances. So, it is in virtue of having the same mental make-up, so to speak, that my aesthetic judgement of a particular object demands your and all other subjects' agreement too: if I experience a certain thing in a specific way, then so will you and everyone else because our minds all function in the same fashion. Aesthetic judgements, in this way, have the same normative scope as moral judgements for Kant.

The fact that our experience of beauty is fundamentally pleasurable follows on from this feature of aesthetic appreciation according to Kant, for aesthetic experiences are fundamentally enjoyable precisely because they are not constrained by rules. Judgements about beauty are not based on concepts in the sense that they cannot, as mentioned above, be the result of applying concepts along rule-governed patterns. Instead, such judgements reflect our appreciation of those forms that harmoniously engage our faculties of imagination and understanding in this unconstrained way; they reveal our affinity with those forms that cannot be brought under any definite rule. Our experience of beauty is, then, the outcome of what Kant calls the 'free play' between two of the three main cognitive capacities, namely the imagination and the understanding (the third faculty, of reason, is not engaged), and occurs under the same conditions in all human beings. This is the sense in which a judgement of beauty is autonomous or 'legislates for itself', and is not 'subjected to a heteronomy of laws of experience' (2000: §59; 353).

The autonomy of aesthetic judgements lies at the heart of Kant's account of the relation between beauty and moral goodness. Underlying morality, for Kant, is a rational ideal of autonomy in so far as moral judgements incorporate both subjective responses and the demands of duty. Moral judgements must, in other words, be conceived as the outcome of free individual choice, albeit a choice in accordance with duty where duty is given to us by the universal law of reason. Beauty can, according to Kant, help resolve this seeming incompatibility: the experience of beauty is a symbol of morality precisely because the freedom of the imagination (which ensures the 'free play') is the only experience in which any form of freedom – including the freedom of the will so central to moral deliberation and judgement – can become tangible to us.

As Kant sees it, beauty thus gives sensible form to moral ideas (2000: §60; 356); the symbolic presentation of the idea of morality through the experience of beauty is the only form available for the presentation of moral ideas to sense because, on Kant's account, moral ideas cannot in themselves be presented to the senses (because they are purely rational ideas). Through the experience of beauty, in other words, we are given a sensible representation of the relation between reason and feeling in morality. Ultimately, judgements about beauty are symbols of moral freedom itself. Beauty is the symbol of morality for Kant, then, because the experience of beauty can count as an experience of moral freedom, and that freedom lies at the very heart of morality itself.

It is clear even from a brief outline of Kant's theory such as this one that beauty is deeply embedded in the broader metaphysical and epistemological framework of the *Critique of the Power of Judgement*. For Kant, as for Plato and Socrates before him, the basic goal of all philosophy is a moral one. The question of how to live well and act for the best is that which underwrites our enquiry into the nature of the world and the minds of those who inhabit it. Kant's entire critical project, his transcendental system of knowledge, consists in the attempt to reconcile the sphere of human action with the natural workings of the world (or, as Kant puts it, the 'great gulf' that separates the concept of nature from the concept of freedom (2000: Introduction, IX), a project guided ultimately by the belief that the natural goodness implicit in the idea of God's creation must be immanent to human reason.

If human morality and the idea of our coming to know and understand the nature of the good, then, is the presiding concept for Kant's philosophy, we can see even from the brief discussion above that the idea of beauty stands in an important – even crucial – relation to this morality. For if the means by which we come to perceive beauty are the same as the means by which we come to perceive the good as a state of affairs to be desired; and if, further, our perception of beauty is necessary to our coming to perceive things or courses of action as good, then it is certainly clear that there is a great deal more at stake in the notion of aesthetic taste than the question, say, of why we may prefer a certain painting or piece of music to another. Beauty, for Kant, lies very much at the heart of the matter. Nor can the sense in which beauty is construed as 'symbolic' of morality be taken as having anything in common with the trivial idea that beauty might symbolize morality as a result of convention. The symbolic relation Kant infers lies, as we have seen, deep inside our mental faculties.

We can now see that that the two strands of Kant's account that we began by distinguishing are far from detached from one another in any particularly significant sense. The fact that both moral and aesthetic judgements are autonomous provides Kant with the material to get the analogy going, as it were, and the claim that the experience of beauty is a 'propaedeutic' to moral feeling is its result.

Another important aspect of Kant's understanding is the normative status of both moral and aesthetic judgements. Thus, my judgement that a particular course of action is the right one is both autonomous – the judgement answers to nothing other than reason for authority – and prescriptive: the course of action is held to be right for all other subjects in the same situation. Similarly, my judgement that some object is beautiful is both autonomous (on the basis of my pleasure in experiencing the harmonious free-play of my understanding and imagination) and held to be valid for all other subjects, on the grounds that our perception of beauty occurs at the level of the very structure of our mental faculties, and thus is a sense common to all, or a 'sensus communis', as Kant calls it.

The fact that, for Kant, aesthetic judgements are not just idiosyncratic, personal responses, but are held to be generally valid is often found to be problematic by those who argue that aesthetic taste should be a purely personal matter. Without seeking to address this controversy in its full complexity, Kant's view on this question relates to his understanding of beauty as the symbol of morality. For clearly, it is necessary for Kant to uphold the general validity of moral judgements on the grounds that such judgements are subject to nothing other than reason. To hold that beauty is the symbol (in a non-trivial sense) of morality, it follows that the same general validity must also hold for aesthetic judgements as well. Clearly, too, it is important to bear in mind in this respect that Kant claims the pleasure we experience in the perception of beauty derives partly from its giving rise to our awareness of our own moral freedom. The pleasure that we derive from beauty is, in this sense, itself a moral pleasure because it consists in the awareness of ourselves as moral subjects. Thus, there is more at stake in Kant's claims in respect of the prescriptive nature of aesthetic judgements than one might at first suppose.

Are we therefore now in a position to solve our query about the logical priority of moral over aesthetic value? Does Kant's analysis of beauty as a symbol of morality establish with certainty that beauty is to be derived from morality in a strong sense? The claim to the effect that beauty serves as a 'propaedeutic' to moral feeling seems in many respects highly plausible. Indeed, as we shall see in the following chapter, this area of Kant's thought on the matter has perhaps proved the most fruitful in terms of subsequently philosophical positions on the moral status of aesthetic value and experience. The claim seems to hold if we consider individual and local cases, such as the way in which the idea of forgiveness often seems beautiful. It might be the case, then, that the practice of experiencing beauty itself leads to forgiveness. Alternatively, we might restrict the claim even further to the observation that, since a large portion of artistic endeavour has been centred around the representation of moral and religious exemplars – and since this representation has been characterized by beauty – that our sense of beauty has become conventionally orientated towards the moral qualities that our culture and its history have praised.

While these are plausible if somewhat restricted claims, Kant's analysis operates at a deeper epistemological level than this. He argues that an aesthetic judgement consists at bottom in the operation of valuing an object in and of itself (as opposed to valuing on the basis of some determinate concept one might have in respect of the object's function), and that it is at this structural level that the preparation for and attunement of moral sensibility lies. This is because, as we saw briefly above, the idea of human morality is for Kant contingent on the understanding of our actions and other people in themselves rather than in terms of their effects or uses.

When we make a moral judgement – about, say, whether we should adopt our deceased friend's child – then that judgement, according to Kant, should be based solely on reasonable considerations concerning the idea of adoption in general and particular, and should be made independently of, say, a desire on our part to adopt a child for reasons of wanting to start a family. Similarly, when we make an aesthetic judgement about the beauty, say, of a sunset, then, according to Kant, the beautiful sensation that we experience in making that judgement has nothing to do with our suspicion that the sunset heralds fine weather for our garden party on the following day, but, rather, has everything to do with our mental faculties' engagement with the sunset itself, or rather with its form. But because such a pure aesthetic judgement consists simply and solely in the particular kind of pleasure associated with the free play of the faculties, and because this free play arises solely through the consideration of things in themselves, the experience of beauty trains the mind to find pleasure in the exercise of moral judgements too. In other words, although our moral judgements are made on the basis of reason alone, the cultivation of our aesthetic sensibilities will encourage us to find pleasure in the making of such moral judgements.

This viewpoint certainly seems coherent if one accepts Kant's system as a whole, something it is beyond our current context to try to assess here. However, the problems associated with Immoralism in Part II still seem to raise serious difficulties for Kant's analysis. Indeed, because Kant commits himself both to the view that aesthetic judgements enjoy the same normative status and general validity as moral judgements – that is to say, an aesthetic precept no less than a moral one permits of a kind of universal correctness – and to the view that the beautiful symbolizes the good, then he is bound to the view that morally corrupt artworks are bound to be ugly. That is to say, for Kant, if we truly know something or someone to be bad, we cannot but find that aspect of it that we judge to be bad anything other than ugly. The same would go for beauty. In realizing something or someone to be good, we are bound to find that which in it or them we deem good to be beautiful.

One's assessment of Kant's position here stands or falls with one's subscription to the whole of his transcendental critical system. Nonetheless, without suggesting either that this system, in which goodness and beauty are intricately linked, trumps the Immoralist counter-claim, or that it is rendered irrelevant by this claim's persistence, we should not be put off from exploring the fruitful lines of enquiry suggested by the more modest parts of the Kantian package. For, regardless of whether we find the operation to be bound by the transcendental unity of human freedom and the laws of nature, there is still something to be gained from considering that the experience of beauty may lead to, as Kant put it, a 'mental attunement favorable to moral feeling'.

Moreover, the idea that a person's propensity to take an interest in beauty is said to be suggestive of 'a good soul' (2000: §42; 298–9) seems to enjoy a life independently of the immediate sphere of Kantian philosophy. Both of these claims, and the question of their significance when considered independently of Kant's underlying theory of beauty as the symbol of morality, will be at the heart of our investigation in the following two chapters. Thus in Chapter 7 we will investigate the epistemological aspect of our concern – namely, that our judgements of beauty predispose us to greater consideration and sensitivity in our moral judgements – in the light of a number of subsequent theories about the nature of aesthetic sensibility and its relation to moral sensibility. In Chapter 8, on the other hand, where we shall turn to consider the ancient idea of the beauty of the soul, we shall be more concerned with the psychological and metaphysical aspects that can be understood to extend from Kant's analysis.

THE SUBLIME

One aspect of Kant's conception of aesthetic judgement that we have so far not considered is his notion of the sublime. At first sight, Kant's notion of the sublime would seem to permit of a more expansive moral application than that of beauty. This is because, unlike the fairly localized experience of beauty as a form of pleasure that arises in response to certain objects, the experience of the sublime leads one, for Kant, to consider oneself in comparison to one's (usually natural) environment; and part of the comparative consideration involves reflection on one's status as a free, moral agent. To judge some object of sight or sound sublime is, for Kant, to experience a feeling of awe and wonder sufficient to cause one to consider oneself in relation to this object of the experience, to weigh oneself against it, as it were (2000: §24–26).

The category of the sublime, then, while nonetheless clearly related, is paradigmatically distinct from that of beauty. For whereas beauty is characterized by a harmonious resonating of one's faculties with the object of aesthetic awareness, this harmony is absent from our experience of the sublime. Typically for Kant, a judgement of the sublime occurs in response to the vastness or dynamism of nature – to an expanse of sea, say, or a mountain range. And whereas a judgement of the beautiful would occur from our perception of the form of something, with the sublime we glimpse the form but are unable to comprehend it. The object of aesthetic awareness, that is to say, seems to be such that it overwhelms the imagination's capacity to comprehend it. In this situation, Kant argues, our imagination will strive to comprehend the object in accordance with a demand of reason, but fails to do so (2000: §25–26).

Although the experience of the sublime is bound to a cognitive failure in this respect, it is nonetheless characterized by a form of pleasure. This pleasure, triggered off by (or expressive of) this lack of harmony in our faculties, is held to consist primarily in our becoming aware of the power and autonomy of our minds. Confronted by the incalculable, as it were, the mind seems to rise to the challenge, not by overcoming the mathematical or perceptual obstacles in comprehending the form of the object of aesthetic awareness, but in simply becoming reflectively aware of the equally limitless power that our minds must be endowed with in order to meet nature half way, so to speak.

In this manner, Kant argues that just as beauty is the symbol of morality, the sublime is a symbol of the power of practical reason, for the experience of the sublime consists in a feeling of the superiority of our own power of reason, as a super-sensible faculty, over nature (2000: §28; 261). By extension, therefore, the idea of the sublime is, for Kant, strongly connected to our morality in general because it brings us into sensible contact with our faculty of reason, which is the source of moral knowledge. In addition, Kant holds that the sense of respect for the natural world that the experience of the sublime generates is akin to the sense of respect out of which we deduce and strive to fulfil our moral duties.

Arguably, then, the Kantian category of the sublime is a better candidate for an exploration of the intersection between aesthetic and moral value than the beautiful, for the reason that the faculty of reason is engaged in judgement or perception of the sublime in a way that it is left unemployed in a judgement or perception of the beautiful. That is to say, we are – at least potentially – directly engaging our moral faculties when we contemplate the sublime, something that is necessarily not the case with our awareness of beauty.

Nonetheless, it is fair to say that for our purposes Kant's idea of beauty seems a more fruitful line of enquiry. This is not solely because Kant's treatment of the idea of the sublime seems rather less systematically worked through than his treatment of beauty. Rather, it is because the sublime is characterized principally by a form of awareness of the faculties on which our morality is based, rather than by a form of mental operation which also lies at the heart of moral judgement. That is to say, the sublime brings us into contact with what amounts to the source and possibility of our morality, rather than into contact with the moral sphere itself, with which it seems to be connected neither in terms of sensibility nor in terms of structure of the mental operation. For this reason, although we should certainly not exclude the sublime from consideration, it is primarily with extensions of the idea of beauty with which the following two chapters will be concerned.

SCHILLER ON AESTHETIC AND MORAL EDUCATION

Before we move on to the theories of aesthetic and moral sensibility examined in the next chapter, we should turn briefly to consider one of the earliest critics of Kant's analysis of aesthetic judgements. Five years after the emergence of Kant's *Critique of the Power of Judgement*, the poet, dramatist and theorist Friedrich Schiller published his *Letters on the Aesthetic Education of Man*. These take the form of an investigation into the nature and significance of man's engagement with the arts, and aesthetic experience more generally. Thus unlike Kant, for whom the analytic reach of his claims about aesthetic judgement and value consisted primarily in terms of completing his philosophical system as a whole, Schiller is eager to argue more widely for the political and social importance of aesthetic experience and education. In particular, Schiller holds that Kant's claim that aesthetic judgements are a 'propaedeutic' to moral judgements simply does not go far enough.[3] Rather, Schiller contends, man's engagement with art and with the aesthetic can in and of itself transform his relation to his environment. The reach of the effects of artistic experience are thus political and social as well as moral.

Schiller's main claim is rooted in the observation that 'it is only through Beauty that man makes his way to Freedom' (1993: 90). The experience of beauty, for Schiller, is thus a necessary step in man's achievement of morality and its realization in political justice. The implication, therefore, is that the cultivation of taste through aesthetic education itself leads to human self-fulfilment in the political and social spheres, which Schiller understood to be extensions of the moral realm. In this respect, then, Schiller seems to go a great deal further in his claims for the moral value of aesthetic experience than Kant. For while Kant maintained a deep epistemological and metaphysical connection between moral and aesthetic value, and our experience of them, the exercise of our sensibility was not for him necessary in order for someone to enter in the moral sphere, since, by its nature, the moral sphere is grounded perfectly in reason.

Schiller presents the problem to be solved by his concept of aesthetic education in several ways, and although the moral application is at the heart of his theory, he addresses it primarily as a political rather than a moral problem. In his sixth Letter, he offers a powerful diagnosis of late-eighteenth-century society in which the characteristic problem is analysed in terms of the alienation of the individual and the increasing fragmentation of the social or political group.

Schiller sees the growth in man's isolation from the wider community as a modern development, related to increasing remoteness of government from the concerns of everyday life. With strong echoes of Rousseau, Schiller argues that the increase in systematic but instrumental rationality and bureaucracy at the heart of the modern idea of government has had the effect of isolating citizens. The state, he proclaims, 'remains forever a stranger to its citizens; at no point does it ever make contact with their feelings' (1993: 99–100). In turn, the individual citizens respond by emphasizing their individual well-being at the expense of any consideration of the wider well-being of the community and society in general.

At the same time, strongly anticipating Marx's analysis of capitalism, Schiller observes an increase in the identification of the citizen with his or her economic output. He writes:

[M]aterial needs reign supreme and bend a degraded humanity beneath their tyrannical yoke. Utility is the great idol of our age, to which all powers are in thrall and to which all talent must pay homage. (1993: 89)

Social and political forces are therefore held responsible for diminishing man's moral awareness by reducing individual consciousness to a consideration of one's economic function as a mere cog in the machine.

The importance of the cultivation of aesthetic sensibility, and of aesthetic and artistic experience more generally, is understood in terms of acting as a palliative for society's modern ills. The primary sense in which aesthetic experience is understood in this way is in terms of its acting to restore a sense of harmony to human society and a greater nobility to human desires. Developing Kant's understanding that the aesthetic judgement derived from and encouraged the tendency to consider things in themselves, regardless of their utility value, Schiller argues that beauty leads directly toward an ennobling of human desire. In other words, he looks to aesthetic education to provide a 'total revolution of man's whole way of feeling', in the hope that this would lead to a renaissance in political economy, and a re-alignment of government away from hard economic concerns and back, as he saw it, toward a more integrated focus on the moral health of the social group.

At first sight, then, it would seem that Schiller's theory of aesthetic education has a wider moral reach than that of Kant. Nonetheless, and bearing in mind the difficulties implicit in Kant's text, it seems arguable that Schiller's contribution consists essentially in a more politically charged amplification of Kant's essential claim that the structure of aesthetic judgement leads to the consideration of things in themselves as something beneficial to moral sensibility and clear moral reasoning. Indeed, fascinating, far-ranging and ambitious though Schiller's programme of aesthetic revolution is, it would seem to stand or fall (and stand or fall rather heavily) on our acceptance of this analysis of Kant's, something which, as we saw, it seems difficult to assess independently of a subscription to Kant's philosophical system in general. It seems, in other words, for the purposes of our present context, that Schiller's contribution leads in the same direction as Kant's, namely to an investigation of the nature of aesthetic sensibility and its relation to our moral faculties.

PRELIMINARY CONCLUSIONS: BRIDGING THE GULF

Kant's aesthetic theory, deeply embedded in his greater philosophical project, has no lesser aim than to provide a conceptual bridge across the deep conceptual division between the realm of human freedom and action and that of the law of nature. Far from offering a restricted account of the vagaries of human taste, Kant incorporates such an account in a systematic theory conceived ultimately in terms of explaining the meaning and purpose of human existence. It is in this light that the moral extension of the aesthetic sphere may best be grasped. For while, in itself, there is nothing necessarily moral for Kant about our ability to perceive and reflect upon aesthetic qualities, this ability nonetheless provides our only means of obtaining a sensuous illustration of moral ideas. That is to say, although moral ideas answer solely to the faculty of reason (which is not directly employed in aesthetic perception and judgement), the experience of valuing an object of experience solely for its own sake central to the phenomenon of beauty mirrors the structure of moral judgements; and, in so doing, it provides a crucial connection for Kant between the realm of feeling and sensibility and that of reason. Our ability to grasp beauty thus comes, for Kant, to symbolize morality because it is the primary means through which we come to know what goodness feels like, as it were.

Although Schiller's contribution is framed as a criticism and revision of Kant's analysis, as we have seen, the *Letters on Aesthetic Education* really offer a political and social extension of Kant's basic analysis. In this, although it shows clearly that beauty's being a 'symbol of morality' is not limited to the extremely general terms in which Kant frames it, but rather extends to the workings of government and society, it is still dependent on our acceptance of that Kantian package in its entirety.

However, one of the most important lessons we can draw independently from both Schiller's and Kant's account of beauty as the symbol of morality is the idea that there might be some significant parallels between the sensitivity we exercise in aesthetic and moral experience respectively. This conception that the mental abilities we employ in discerning beauty and aesthetic character are related to or the same as those which we use to discern the moral quality and character of things has proved to be one of the most fruitful and consistently used aspects of the Kantian contribution to the debate. Let us therefore now consider this idea of our sensibility to moral and aesthetic value in more detail.

CHAPTER 7

SENSIBILITY TO VALUE

HOW IS AESTHETIC CHARACTER ASSESSED?

As we have seen, the process of engaging appropriately with an artwork involves setting in motion a whole range of mental operations. These operations draw, more or less directly, on relatively complex sets and combinations of cognitive and affective abilities, such as imagination, understanding, perception, sensitivity, taste and reason. In other words, when we listen to Mozart's *C minor Fantasy* or look at Cézanne's *Card Players*, for example, we are not just exercising our hearing or vision. Instead, we put to use an entire gamut of skills which enable us to grasp not only the visual or audible character of the artwork under scrutiny, but also the symbolism of the depicted scene, the mood which it expresses, the feelings undergone by the characters, references made by the artist to events or persons beyond that particular work, and much more. To properly appreciate an artwork's overall character, then, it seems that we must activate several psychological abilities that, together, provide us with the 'key', so to speak, to the adequate experience of a particular work or object of aesthetic appreciation. For in experiencing an artwork *qua* artwork, we ought to address every aspect of that work's character: emotional, intellectual, aesthetic, moral, humorous, and perhaps more.

That we employ a good deal of these abilities in relation to the more cognitive aspects of artistic experience will not seem surprising. After all, the critical interpretation of an abstract painting or the deciphering of a poem's hidden meaning, say, is not all that dissimilar to some other (non-artistic) pursuits such as map-reading or attempting to determine someone else's intentions in some or other non-propositional form or expression, a gesture for example: both kinds of activities involve analytic thought-processes and, as such, require the exercise of most (if not all) of the abilities mentioned above. In other words, to appreciate T. S. Eliot's *The Lovesong of J. Alfred Prufrock* appropriately, we use our imagination to conjure up and envisage the yellow smoke that the author describes, our under-standing to grasp how blasé and tired the narrator is of his own life, our sensitivity to discern his growing despair, and our reason in order to interpret and extrapolate more general lessons and axioms from the poem.

It may nonetheless be argued that this model cannot explain all facets of artistic experience. What, one may ask, of the more dis-tinctively aesthetic side of artistic experience; what of the discern-ment of aesthetic character? As previous chapters have shown, aesthetic qualities, despite their heterogeneity, constitute a category of qualities distinct from non-aesthetic qualities, and so we must be able to explain how such qualities are discerned and assessed. What is more, if there were nothing to aesthetic assess-ment that could not be captured by our ordinary perceptual abilities, then how do we account for those among us who have perfectly operative ordinary senses yet seemingly no aesthetic sense?[1] How, then, are we to account for the way in which we come to grasp the harmony, elegance, dynamism, ugliness or heaviness of a particular artwork?

Three principal avenues seem available to us in the attempt to determine the nature of our perception and experience of specifi-cally aesthetic qualities. First, aesthetic perception and cognition could function rather like the discernment of colour or mere sound. After all, at least some aesthetic qualities seem to be immediately apparent to us in somewhat the same way that redness or the high pitch of a scream tends to be. Garishness, for example, seems to require little more than redness does in order to be perceived. Second, aesthetic perception and cognition could require a special faculty, a unique mental ability exercised for the sole purpose of picking out and judging aesthetic character. Beauty and ugliness, at the very least, do seem sufficiently exceptional in comparison to other qualities to require some distinctive kind of 'knack', so to speak, in order to be grasped and assessed. Third, aesthetic percep-tion and cognition could be said to parallel the moral case in that at least some aesthetic qualities seem to demand a sensibility to evaluative features in many respects similar to that built into moral sensitivity. The perception and assessment of stylishness, refine-ment or elegance, say, does seem to call for a susceptibility and responsiveness not all that unlike the one employed in the discern-ment of tactfulness or scrupulousness, for example.

In many ways, the question before us lies at the very heart of philosophical aesthetics. For without a satisfactory account of aesthetic perception and cognition we lack the tools to explain not only *how* we assess aesthetic character and ascribe aesthetic qualities to things, persons and events, but also *why* we do so. That is to say, if we cannot clarify the manner in which we make aesthetic judgements, we most probably won't be able to justify that practice in the first place; if no acceptable explanation can be provided of our methodology, then we might not even have the resources to establish that there is indeed some aesthetic quality or character capable of grounding aesthetic appreciation as we know it.

The epistemology of aesthetic judgement is difficult to disentangle partly because the nature of aesthetic experience and aesthetic value seems, as we have seen repeatedly, to vary so greatly from case to case. Some objects of aesthetic appreciation may seem to appeal directly to our emotions (e.g. Shakespeare's *Romeo and Juliet*) whereas others (e.g. Yves Klein's monochrome blue paintings) do not; some require a certain kind of intellectual effort (e.g. Schoenberg's Second Chamber Symphony) whereas others (e.g. Brancusi's *Bird*) do not. Moreover, different artworks appeal to different perceptual senses or combinations thereof, and it is not always easy to tell which sense is called for in a particular artistic context. Nevertheless, two things can be said with certainty about the discernment of aesthetic character.

In a first instance, aesthetic judgements are essentially perceptual judgements in so far as they must be based on the subject's first-hand perceptual experience. Making an aesthetic judgement on the back of someone else's testimony, say, simply disqualifies that judgement from being genuinely aesthetic. It is not, in other words, because one's friend, say, deems a certain artwork beautiful that one can oneself make the judgement that that work is indeed beautiful.[2] Rather, a judgement such as 'That is a graceful sculpture' or 'This is an unbalanced painting' must be founded on the judgement-maker's personal perceptual experience of that particular work. That is to say, an aesthetic judgement has to be grounded in one's own first-hand perception of aesthetic character.[3]

The second axiom is clearly related to the first: in much the same way as the making of an aesthetic judgement must be based on our own individual experience, aesthetic judgement must also be non-inferential. As was discussed in Chapter 6 in relation to Kant's theory, there are no rules for aesthetic value – it is not because the last painting that I saw depicting yellow flowers in a yellow vase was balanced and harmonious that I can automatically ascribe those aesthetic qualities to the next painting I see with yellow flowers in a yellow vase. As Kant explained in his *Critique of the Power of Judgement*, aesthetic judgements are autonomous; there are no principles of aesthetic taste that can be applied and said to guarantee the production of a certain aesthetic character.

Now, a commitment to the two closely related tenets outlined above does not necessarily entail a particular position on the issue we began this chapter by raising, namely what kind of psychological ability (or set thereof) we put to use in aesthetic discernment and judgement-making. For the claim that aesthetic judgements are fundamentally perceptual and non-inferential does not bind one to equating aesthetic discernment with colour perception, or to positing a unique mental faculty. Nor, again, does it suggest necessarily that we should follow the model of moral awareness and sensitivity. It is important to note, nevertheless, that all these accounts actually rely on a commitment to the perceptual and non-inferential nature of aesthetic judgements.

There are, however, other good grounds to exclude the first of these options as a viable solution to our concern. Because although colour judgements are perceptual and non-inferential too, the aesthetic case permits of considerably more complexity than this alleged counterpart. Even if certain aesthetic qualities can resemble colour properties experientially in so far as both can be perceptually immediate (we can, after all, be 'struck' or taken aback by certain aesthetic qualities in a similar way that we can be with an expanse of colour, say), aesthetic qualities can be seen to be metaphysically dependent on a whole array of other features in a way that colour properties are not. An aesthetic quality such as elegance, for example, will depend for its manifestation and existence on other (often non-aesthetic) qualities such as the shape of a brush-stroke, the symmetrical relation between parts, a good use of the light, a certain arrangement of positions, angles and shades, and, moreover, the way in which all these features interact. What is more, the presence of aesthetic qualities is a very delicate matter to the extent that the very slightest alteration in a work's non-aesthetic qualities can change that work's aesthetic character beyond recognition. After all, it takes no more than a small variation of the brush-stroke's line or a minute rearrangement of an angle for the work to lose its elegant character.

Clearly, none of this really applies to the case of colour: the yellowness of Van Gogh's *Sunflowers* is not ontologically dependent on several of the work's other features, nor is it going to vanish or change completely simply because of an alteration of another of the work's characteristics. So, although aesthetic perception certainly involves direct sense-perception, just like colour or sound, the employment of such perceptual abilities is only the starting-point of the process that constitutes aesthetic discernment and assessment.

On closer inspection, then, there seem to be two possible models of explanation of how we discern and assess distinctively aesthetic character. Either there is such a thing as one special sensibility exclusively concerned with aesthetic character, or, alternatively, there is a form of awareness and responsiveness similar to the one we exercise in moral discernment and judgement. Let us now take a closer look at these two possibilities.

AESTHETIC SENSIBILITY – IDENTIFYING TERMS AND CONCEPTS

If the process underlying the making of aesthetic judgement is to be accounted for in terms of one unique mental faculty – aesthetic sensibility – several problematic aspects of our aesthetic epistemology can be clarified and explained. First and foremost, aesthetic sensibility can make sense of how it is that we seem fully capable of perceiving aesthetic character in every kind of thing around us and on a daily basis even though there are so many ways in which that character can take form and be expressed. As long as it is a distinctively *aesthetic* quality, one may thus argue, it can be grasped with the help of our specifically *aesthetic* sensibility – that, so to speak, is what aesthetic sensibility does.

In a second instance, positing a unique aesthetic mental faculty can shed light on exactly how our ordinary mental abilities are involved in aesthetic perception and cognition. In other words, we don't need to worry about how our ordinary mental abilities, when placed in an aesthetic context, suddenly seem capable of grasping an entirely different kind of quality without further help and assistance – our theory of aesthetic sensibility would also explain that too.

The attempt to account for our aesthetic epistemology in terms of a special faculty is not an entirely novel enterprise. In fact, Kant's entire aesthetic theory relies on such a notion: in the third *Critique*, the faculty of aesthetic taste is said to be 'the faculty for judging an object or a kind of representation through a satisfaction or dissatisfaction', and the object of this representation is that which 'is called beautiful'.[4] For Kant, then, aesthetic judgement can only be the direct outcome of the exercise of this faculty; aesthetic perception and cognition simply cannot get started without it.

The suggestion that the discernment of aesthetic character is to be explained by appealing to a unique psychological ability thus seems to stand in good stead: not only does it seem well-grounded for the two reasons outlined above; it also has a formidable proponent in Kant.

One more recent influential theory based on the idea that there is a separate faculty of aesthetic sensibility which accounts for the making of aesthetic judgements is that developed by Frank Sibley. In his seminal article 'Aesthetic Concepts', Sibley begins his argument by highlighting the fact that we all tend to talk about artworks in many different ways. Generally speaking, Sibley writes, our comments can be divided into two broad categories. On the one hand,

> [w]e say that a novel has a great number of characters and deals with life in a manufacturing town; that a painting uses pale colours, predominantly blues and greens, and has kneeling figures in the foreground; that the theme in a fugue is inverted at such a point and that there is a stretto at the close; that the action of a play takes place in the span of one day and that there is a reconciliation scene in the fifth act. (2001a: 1)

Remarks such as these, Sibley writes, can be made by 'anyone with normal eyes, ears, and intelligence'. We do not, in other words, need any special faculty beyond our ordinary psychological abilities in order to discern and assess these features. Then again,

[w]e also say that a poem is tightly-knit or deeply moving; that a picture lacks balance, or has a certain serenity and repose, or that the grouping of the figures sets up an exciting tension; that the characters in a novel never really come to life, or that a certain episode strikes a false note. (2001a: 1)

That is to say, in addition to the first kind of comment, we also make remarks that pick out a work's specifically aesthetic qualities. According to Sibley, the distinction between these two kinds of comments lies precisely in the kind of ability that we need to employ in order to discern the different kinds of qualities. So, whereas the making of the latter kind of judgement 'requires the exercise of taste, perceptiveness, or sensitivity, of aesthetic discrimination or appreciation . . . one would not say this of my first group' (2001a: 1).

Sibley thus draws a line between terms and expressions that do call for the employment of aesthetic sensibility to be perceived, and terms and expressions that do not. But Sibley does not leave the matter at that. Rather, he takes the point further still by concluding that 'when a word or expression is such that [aesthetic] taste or perceptiveness is required in order to apply it, I shall call it an aesthetic term or expression, and I shall, correspondingly, speak of aesthetic concepts' (2001a: 1).

What we are provided with here, then, is nothing short of a definition: for Sibley, a term or concept is aesthetic if and only if its application requires the exercise of aesthetic sensibility. In other words, aesthetic sensibility, or, to be more precise, its employment, is that which sets aesthetic terms and concepts apart from non-aesthetic terms and concepts.

Again, there is nothing about Sibley's theory that stands at odds with the two tenets of aesthetic judgement outlined above – quite the contrary, in fact. First of all, for Sibley, aesthetics 'deals with a certain kind of perception' (2001b: 34). In discerning aesthetic character, we have to '*see* the grace or unity of a work, *hear* the plaintiveness or frenzy in the music, *notice* the gaudiness of a colour scheme, *feel* the power of a novel, its mood, or its certainty of tone'. What is more, to think that 'one can make aesthetic judgements without aesthetic perception, say, by following rules of some kind, is to misunderstand aesthetic judgement' (2001b: 34). Thus, in common with Kant, Sibley's characterization of aesthetic judgement and the perception of specifically aesthetic qualities is rooted in personal experience and, although it draws on our intellectual faculties, does so in a necessarily non-inferential manner. On closer scrutiny, however, the way in which Sibley conceives of aesthetic sensibility and the philosophical work he expects it to perform within his aesthetic theory encounters some serious philosophical objections. Three accusations seem particularly challenging.

First, any attempt to define aesthetic qualities in terms of (the exercise of) an aesthetic sensibility (and vice versa) is circular. For what explanatory resources are really available to us if the category of aesthetic qualities is to be accounted for by aesthetic sensibility, and aesthetic sensibility, in turn, is described as that which picks out aesthetic qualities? As Ted Cohen (1973) has pointed out, what is needed here is some principled way of settling which concepts and terms are distinctively aesthetic that does *not* appeal to a notion which already contains the term 'aesthetic'. If this cannot be done, then no acceptable definition can be had since the notion at the very heart of this puzzle – the aesthetic – figures both in that which we are trying to explain (the *'explanandum'*) as well as in that by means of which we are attempting to explain it (the *'explanans'*).

Second, how exactly are we to understand this special faculty through which aesthetic qualities are to be individuated? In the words of Peter Kivy, aesthetic terms, for Sibley, are those that 'require for their application an ability over and above the capacities of mind and body that mark a person out as "normal"' (1975: 198). Or, as David Broiles has pointed out, aesthetic taste for Sibley is 'an ability to see or discern a type of quality not available to a person solely on the basis of his possessing normal eyes, ears, and intelligence. It is on a par with the five senses . . . so that just as some people are deaf, some others lack taste' (1964: 221). Yet to the question of what this aesthetic sensibility is supposed to be constituted by, Sibley fails to give a satisfactory answer: although he defines the ability as something beyond the normal he does not tell us what that non-normal aspect of aesthetic sensibility actually amounts to.

Third, and finally for our purposes, it may be held that aesthetic qualities acquire a rather strange and dubious ontological status on Sibley's account. By claiming that aesthetic qualities require –

for their perception – a special kind of faculty, such qualities are automatically set apart from more ordinary ones. All we are told, it seems, is that aesthetic qualities are different from other qualities in so far as they call for the exercise of a different mental ability that seems to operate rather like an intuition. And as with most kinds of quality to be understood in terms of some form of intuition, aesthetic qualities seem to become more and more difficult to account for philosophically.[5]

These three difficulties raise serious issues of genuine concern for any attempt to delineate the aesthetic by appealing to a special aesthetic perceptual faculty: the circularity of the definition, the lack of detailed explanation of what aesthetic sensibility really is and the non-natural character of aesthetic qualities are not insignificant worries. Left as they are, they certainly put an end to any serious aspirations such a theory may have to be fruitful and adequate.

That is not to say, however, that we should lose sight of what it is that such theories have to offer. Given the difficulties with establishing exactly how and with what psychological ability (or set thereof) we discern and assess aesthetic character, it is clear that the positing of a specific faculty would have a great deal of explanatory reach. For even though, as we have already established, our more ordinary mental abilities are involved in aesthetic perception and cognition, something more must be said about grasping distinctively *aesthetic* character. Obviously, one cannot simply conjure up a new mental faculty for every kind of quality that one needs to account for philosophically. But the way in which aesthetic sensibility seems to be something one can develop and refine suggests that aesthetic awareness or perceptiveness is at the very least a form of competence or experience-based aptitude that one can be more or less proficient at. Why, after all, should we be shy to call that a special ability?

If aesthetic sensibility theories are to be successful, then, the problems mentioned – and above all the problem of circularity – would need to be solved with regards to the precise nature and definition of this alleged faculty. For, were an effective definition of aesthetic qualities to be found, the idea of a specific perceptual faculty for picking out such qualities would prove an invaluable model for exploring the way in which our aesthetic sensibilities can be refined, educated and altered. Given its explanatory reach, therefore, although it does not seem possible merely to assert the existence of this special perceptual faculty, on a metaphorical level at the very least it would appear to be an instructive and useful investigative model to employ.

SENSE OF BEAUTY AND MORAL SENSE

Regardless of whether aesthetic sensibility is an innate talent or a purely acquired skill, it is possible to educate ourselves in the role of aesthetic perceivers and assessors. The point applies both to the aesthetic appreciation of art and nature – we can train ourselves to see beauty or other aesthetic qualities in a seascape or landscape just as well as in a painting or a poem. It is possible, for example, to learn to become more discerning of the way in which sunrays can light up the sky in a particularly striking way, or the manner in which waves can roll up on a beach softly and gracefully. Besides repeated experience, one method by which one can accelerate the development of one's aesthetic sensibility is learning how to draw, sculpt, or play an instrument: by acquiring certain skills one can come to perceive certain aspects of a scenery, say, that one had not been able to see before and thus refine one's proficiency at discerning it in the future. Similarly, one can become better and better at grasping the aesthetic qualities of atonal music or expressionist paintings, say. One can, in other words, improve one's aesthetic sensibility and come to grasp aesthetic characteristics that one hadn't even been aware of previously.

Of particular relevance to our concern in this chapter is the fact that this feature of our epistemology is one that the aesthetic case shares with its moral counterpart. Our moral sense – our sense of what is morally right, wrong, suitable, unsuitable, etc. – is developed and refined throughout our lives. From our very youngest childhood to our old age, we continue to increase and expand our ability to discern and assess moral character. In principle at least, we make progress in grasping a moral situation or resolving a moral dilemma appropriately; we get better and better at discerning malicious behaviour, fair treatments, and just courses of action. What in everyday language we refer to as 'moral maturity' is centred around this kind of sensibility to a thing, person or event's moral features.

Aesthetic and moral sensibility thus seem to unfold along parallel lines in so far as both can continuously be improved upon and refined: we can become better and better at grasping the relatively elusive qualities and features that are to be discerned and assessed in aesthetic and moral experience. Answering the question of how aesthetic perception and cognition is to be understood in terms of appealing to the moral case is thus well-grounded in this respect at least, for it counts to the advantage of the suggestion that aesthetic sensibility is to be modelled on moral sensibility that both can accrue and become more sophisticated the more aesthetic and moral experiences we undergo.

Having said that, the claim that assessing aesthetic character is to be accounted for by a comparison with discerning moral character is more often than not taken to imply that the analogy between the two cases is both deeper and more complex than what we have so far described. In fact, defenders of this approach tend to assume that the two kinds of sensibility go hand in hand to the extent that exercising or developing one actually entails exercising or developing the other: to become more perceptive of beauty and gracefulness, say, also leads us to become more aware of and sensitive to moral goodness. Conversely, a diminishing of our sense of empathy, for example, would lead to a corresponding weakening of our aesthetic sensibilities. In this vein, some ecologists have argued that when we engage with our natural environment and come to see how beautiful it really is, we not only come to care for it more but also thereby become morally improved persons.[6] If this is indeed the case, then there may be good grounds to believe that both kinds of sensibility must at least sometimes be exercised simultaneously, so that making a moral judgement can call for both aesthetic and moral sensibility, and similarly in the aesthetic case. To use the words of Marcia Muelder Eaton, '[b]oth aesthetic and moral sensitivity are demanded in making judgements such as "This situation calls for bold action" or "This situation calls for subtlety"' because both 'challenge one to develop powers of perception, reflection, and imagination' (1997: 362).

The picture that is beginning to emerge here, then, is one in which the suggestion that aesthetic sensibility is to be understood in terms of moral sensibility can be cast in such a way as to make the two notions inherently linked both in practice and theory. Two theories that promote this approach to our initial question are the accounts developed in the eighteenth century by Lord Shaftesbury and Francis Hutcheson. As we saw in the preceding chapter, according to Shaftesbury, our sense of beauty is an instance of the very same sensitivity to that order of the universe that is also manifested by the moral sense. The idea, then, is that at some deep level, the qualities our aesthetic and moral sensibilities bring us into perceptual contact with are one and the same: namely, the proper order of the universe, disclosed in which are not only the laws of physics but the moral laws as well.

Following Shaftesbury, Hutcheson refines and bolsters the case by arguing that aesthetic perception is the natural model through which to understand the moral case. Our sense of beauty, he suggests, is a distinct perceptual ability which, although linked to the higher mental faculties, nonetheless operates in the same manner as a sense:

> This superior Power of Perception is justly called a Sense, because of its Affinity to the other Senses in this, that the Pleasure does not arise from any Knowledge of Principles, Proportions, Causes, or the Usefulness of the Object; but strikes us at first with the Idea of Beauty. (2004: 25)

Hutcheson is prepared to identify objectively that in which the paradigmatic aesthetic quality lies: 'the pleasant sensation' through which we know beauty 'arises only from objects in which there is uniformity within variety' (2004: 29). The rule for beauty, in other words, is that, amidst a sensory manifold that is full of change, excitement and contrast, we perceive an order that 'makes sense' of the whole. In addition, Hutcheson claims that our sense of what he calls 'moral beauty' works in precisely the same way. We perceive moral goodness in others, and by extension come to imitate it, by coming to see the natural order that governs their actions. For the 'morally beautiful' person, in other words, there is a unity to their various thoughts, statements and actions that governs them according to a true and natural order. And because, for Hutcheson (as indeed for many other philosophers of this period) true order is intrinsically good, where this judgement is aesthetically correct it is also morally correct. That is to say, where our perception of unity with variety is correct, then we are truly perceiving something good.

For this reason, Hutcheson sees the refinement of our aesthetic sense not only as linked to, but as one and the same thing as, our moral cultivation. Independently of Hutcheson's 'science' of beauty, however, to what extent can we observe this interplay of sensibility? Is it really tenable to claim that aesthetic assessment is inherently linked to moral discernment in this way?

In Chapters 3 and 4, we discussed the idea that some artforms, especially works of literary fiction, can be a source of moral understanding and knowledge. According to Martha Nussbaum (1990), reading great literary works can lead us to acquire an insight into a moral situation that we may well not have gained otherwise. Nussbaum's position thus relies on the possibility that acquiring an understanding of the right way to behave in a particular context or learning to identify a certain kind of personality, say, is dependent upon an artwork's aesthetic features to the extent that only artworks with considerable aesthetic value can be a genuine source of moral knowledge. It is, then, partly because the character is rendered with so much life and that the novel is written in such a stylish and beautiful way that the work can yield the moral knowledge it does.

Despite its advantages, there are some aspects of Nussbaum's account that seem difficult to defend. Is it really the case, one may ask, that *only* great artworks can give us moral understanding, or that it is impossible to grasp certain moral issues without the resources derived from the reading of the great works of literature? Just because the lessons we learn from great literature may be more compellingly presented than those found in, say, second-rate literature, or even our own life experience, does that really make them unique? At the very least, this claim seems a very difficult one to defend.

Nonetheless, Nussbaum's contribution need not be seen as such that it must be bought wholesale. The elements of the theory that draw attention to one of the most important ways in which aesthetic and moral assessment can influence one another seem particularly valuable. For if we accept the claim that the sense of beauty on the one hand, and moral sense on the other, are two intimately related psychological abilities (perhaps even two instances of one and the same faculty), then we certainly have the means to explain the regularly occurring phenomenon that Nussbaum's account is centred on. While this view cannot in and of itself show the suggestion to be correct, it can at the very least indicate that the epistemological relation between aesthetic and moral value exists. There is, in other words, something about grasping the aesthetic qualities of an artwork that is deeply tied in with our ability to discern certain moral features, and vice versa. Since their perception is marked by a particular kind of pleasure, there is after all something compelling about aesthetic qualities, something that appears to confer a sense of rightness to the object. This rightness, in turn, would naturally transfer to our moral sense, making one course of action appear more compelling.

Similarly, our main concern in Chapters 4 and 5 also showed that there are, in fact, many remarkably close connections between the assessment of aesthetic and moral character, for discerning the moral value of a particular artwork can influence our perception of that work's aesthetic value in numerous ways. For example, and least controversially perhaps, the morally flawed world-view promoted by Riefenstahl's film *Triumph of the Will* does seem to affect – and perhaps diminish – the aesthetic value of that film.

However, and despite interactions and philosophical ties such as these, the suggestion that aesthetic perception and cognition is to be accounted for by a close analogy with the moral case does not stand in such a neat and tidy fashion. In reality, counter-examples to the idea that a person with a highly developed aesthetic sensibility must also have a refined moral sense abound, and range from cases such as those relating to the Nazi officers' organization of concerts performed by prisoners in concentration camps to instances of nurses or charity-workers with no sense of appreciation whatsoever for Shakespeare or Wagner.

It seems, then, that aesthetic and moral sensibility do not overlap in the way required for the suggestion under scrutiny here to work out: whereas the former is concerned with aesthetic qualities the latter targets moral qualities, and even though there may be some aesthetic qualities that are value-laden in a way similar to some moral qualities, that is not true of all aesthetic qualities. At its most extreme, there are characters – rather like, say, Gilbert Osmond in Henry James' *Portrait of a Lady* – whose pursuit of aesthetic quality directly leads to moral callousness. The counter-examples, then, just seem too numerous and pressing to allow for a neat and seemingly causal relation.

One possibility worth exploring, then, is that while the perception of gracefulness or garishness calls for a psychological ability that has little if anything in common with that which sets out to grasp fairness or stinginess, discerning beauty and goodness may at bottom share certain features in virtue of the way they feed off each other. That is to say, if it seems dubious that we could neatly tie up the entire gamut of aesthetic and moral qualities, and demonstrate causal relations between our ability to sense the one and the other, we could nonetheless posit a general link between the paradigmatic moral and aesthetic qualities of goodness and beauty of a kind that draws the idea of beauty as an aspect of moral character or personality. We shall turn to this consideration in the following chapter.

PRELIMINARY CONCLUSIONS: AESTHETIC SENSIBILITY AS AN EXPERIENCE-BASED APTITUDE

On reflection, then, surprisingly little philosophical work has been done to add meat to the bones of the epistemological tool with which we assess aesthetic character. In fact, there is a sense in which the more substantial accounts that have been offered are those whereby aesthetic sensibility is understood in terms of an analogy with some other mental ability or proficiency, such as colour perception or moral sensitivity. For despite pinpointing several very important aspects of our aesthetic epistemology and directing us towards what seem to be particularly promising areas of exploration on the issue, the attempt to define aesthetic sensibility as a unique mental faculty is simply not sufficiently informative to do the work that would justify its postulation. Philosophically speaking, then, considerably more would have to be said about the kind of perceptiveness and sensitivity that we employ when we assess aesthetic character and which, to a certain extent, sets our aesthetic experience apart from other kinds of experiences.

As we have seen, part of the reason why the suggestion that aesthetic sensibility is to be conceived in terms of moral sensitivity is that both can be acquired, developed and refined with experience. With experience, aesthetic sensibility can be improved and rendered epistemologically more sophisticated. What we can say with certainty, then, is that aesthetic sensibility is a kind of competence or aptitude to grasp aesthetic qualities and aesthetic character that is fundamentally based on experience in so far as it is through experience that it develops.

What is more, and as both Kant and Sibley have shown, aesthetic judgements are not like expressions of purely personal taste but instead lay claim to a kind of objectivity. In other words, their epistemological status reveals that the ability or competence with which aesthetic qualities are grasped is far from an entirely personal or idiosyncratic skill. For Kant, as we saw in Chapter 6, it is precisely in virtue of stemming from a shared and generally applicable psychological ability that aesthetic judgements can be deemed correct or incorrect.

CHAPTER 8

BEAUTY AND VIRTUE OF THE SOUL

FROM SENSIBILITY TO CHARACTER: TO BE AN AESTHETIC AND MORAL AGENT

When we pursue aesthetic value and seek out aesthetic experience, we give expression to a desire to be exposed to aesthetic qualities such as beauty, serenity, elegance, dynamism, harmony, and perhaps even ugliness. The question of why human beings engage in such pursuits extends far beyond the remit of an aesthetic theory strictly speaking. For any satisfactory answer to that question will have to address broader concerns about the precise nature of the kind of reward we stand to gain from aesthetic experience, the degree to which aesthetic value can be considered autonomous (or not) from other kinds of value, and what the notion of beauty and aesthetic value in general represents or stands for.

The extent to which these concerns call for a direct appeal to moral matters has been the main theme of this book. Is part of the reason why we value aesthetic character and experience that it seems capable of opening our minds to the moral sphere, or of leading to moral understanding more generally? Can the aesthetic value of an artwork be independent of its moral value in so far as assessment and appreciation is concerned? Are the concepts of beauty and aesthetic value inherently linked to that of moral goodness at the very final level of philosophical enquiry? These are the questions that we have examined.

One area of investigation that we have been circling around but left largely untouched so far is that centred around the possibility that our aesthetic aspirations reveal something about the kind of moral agent we are or desire to become. Towards the end of Chapter 7 we reflected on whether aesthetic sensibility is to be conceived as related to moral sense, or even as a kind of instance of moral sensibility. Also, in Chapter 6 we looked at Schiller's theory of aesthetic education and how it can be understood in moral and political terms. In this the final chapter, we will examine the closely related claim that undergoing aesthetic experience and pursuing aesthetic value actually makes one a better moral person – that engaging with aesthetic value leads one to become a superior moral agent.

At least at a first glance, the idea seems perfectly plausible. Notwithstanding the general objections raised toward the end of the last chapter, it nonetheless seems that the better educated we are in the arts and the more apt we become at discerning beauty, the more rounded persons we are in general. Subjecting oneself to aesthetic experience tends to 'open up' one's horizons, so to speak, increase one's field of interest, and render one more aware of some of the less immediately obvious features of the world. More specifically, developing the scope and depth of one's aesthetic sensibility often seems to entail a greater awareness of the higher aims of our actions and thoughts, and perhaps even an improved grasp of how to achieve them. Exposing ourselves to beauty and aesthetic value, in other words, seems to encourage adopting a perspective on the world from which things such as the meaning of life and the pursuit of truth matter more.

One aesthetic theory which rests on the idea that to be a good aesthetic perceiver and judgement-maker requires having certain personality traits is that defended by David Hume. The main aim of Hume's aesthetic theory is to establish a standard of aesthetic taste capable of resolving disputes or disagreements about aesthetic judgements; 'a *Standard of Taste* . . . by which the various sentiments of men may be reconciled; at least a decision afforded confirming one sentiment, and condemning the other' (1965: 5). According to Hume, this standard is to be found in the joint verdict of ideal critics or 'true judges'. In order to be such a judge, Hume argues, five impediments must have been overcome: first, insufficient fineness of discrimination; second, insufficient practice; third, insufficient comparative appreciation of objects of aesthetic appreciation; fourth, insufficient application of means-ends reasoning in assessing such objects; and fifth, prejudice (1965: 16–21). To be a 'true judge', in other words, is to be the kind of person who at the very least aims to be fair-minded and impartial, cultured and knowledgeable, unbiased and balanced, honourable and truthful.

Now clearly, many of these concerns have a distinctively moral flavour, and it is not surprising that the propensity to appreciate aesthetic value has been seen to promote a predilection to pursue moral goals. To be unprejudiced, sensitive, candid and insightful are characteristics we strive to attain not only in relation to aesthetic appreciation but also in moral deliberation. It seems reasonable to presume, moreover, that the acquisition of such traits in one context carries over to other kinds of situation; there is no reason to suppose that being impartial, balanced and fair in aesthetic perception and judgement-making does not also entail an at least partially increased propensity to display those very same traits in processes of moral discernment and assessment as well.

It is a short step from the idea that being an adequate aesthetic perceiver increases the likelihood of also being a good moral judge to the claim that aesthetic experience can play a crucial role in the development of a meaningful life. For if we do indeed gradually become better moral agents by exposing ourselves to aesthetic value, and we grant that moral aspirations are constitutive of a meaningful life, then it follows that aesthetic experience is central to such a life. Aesthetic experience can thus be said to help us to advance in our moral aspirations by preparing the groundwork for moral character through attuning human sensibility to its wider social and moral context.

With this in mind, we can begin to see the broader ramifications of the view discussed in Chapter 3, according to which art can be a source of moral understanding: if, ultimately, yielding moral worth and knowledge is part and parcel of the highest form of human activity, art should be heralded as one of the most important means through which we can accomplish that kind of activity. To use the words of Iris Murdoch, it is through great art that we can

> lose our egoistic personal identity and overcome the divide between subject and object . . . The general notion of a spiritual liberation through art is accessible to common-sense as an account of our relationship to works of art when the walls of the ego fall . . . and we are at one with what we con-template. (1992: 59)

The basics of the process, then, seem well enough established for an unproblematic observation to the effect that artistic and aesthetic experience can and does lead to the development of one's moral character. The question is, though, how far does this process go? Is the experience of beauty to be understood directly in terms of the nurturing of virtue? Does aesthetic value, in other words, lead directly to moral value in terms of the virtue of our own characters, or should the connection be understood more in terms of a general propensity?

THE AESTHETICS OF VIRTUE

The strongest construal of the ontological connectedness of Aesthetics and Morality, or beauty and goodness, takes the form of the assertion that beauty is essentially the appearance of virtue. Instances of this view can be found throughout the history of philosophical aesthetics, but there are three theories that are particularly worth examining in this context. First, there is the account given in its initial philosophical form by Plato. For Plato, the doctrine of the beauty of the soul and the notion of love leads to the idea that true beauty and goodness are inherently linked in character. On this view, we all aspire to and love the beautiful, and to love a beautiful soul is to love the virtuous, for beauty and virtue are one in so far as only a virtuous character can have a beautiful soul. Second, there is Thomas Reid's theory whereby to have an excellent mind is to be truly beautiful. One particularly important feature of such a mind is, precisely, virtue: in order to have an excellent mind one has to be virtuous, and so being virtuous is essential to what it is to be genuinely beautiful. Third, Colin McGinn has developed a version of this, the Aesthetic Theory of Virtue according to which only minds with certain aesthetic qualities can be virtuous. For McGinn, it is impossible for a person's mind to be both vicious and beautiful, or virtuous and ugly.

Let us take a closer look at these theories and reflect upon whether the idea around which they are built may contain the key to the relation between aesthetic and moral value. For if the notions of beauty and goodness, and by extension Aesthetics and Morality, coalesce in the ideal subject of evaluative experience, some of the questions about logical priority and conceptual dependence discussed in Chapter 6 take a more decisive turn.

Most importantly perhaps, the concern about whether beauty is ultimately reducible to moral goodness becomes more pressing, for if what the highest form of the former eventually amounts to is nothing other than the highest form of the latter, then it is a philosophical question of some importance whether there really are two separate notions to examine here in the first place.

Although only a small portion of Plato's work is given to the discussion of art and beauty in general, references to the idea of beauty are a good deal more frequent than is often supposed. From the cosmology and metaphysics of the *Timaeus* to the theory of rhetoric in the *Phaedrus*, the idea of beauty is one that moderates an enormous variety of the objects and themes under discussion. The reason for this is that the idea of beauty, although ultimately without a metaphysical Form itself (or at least not one that mortal intelligence seems able to grasp), is understood paradigmatically as the proper object of human love. Beauty is, by definition, that which we love, or should come to love.

The text in which the subject of love and beauty is addressed most squarely is the *Symposium*. Despite the fact that this dialogue is often overlooked, on account of its perceived lightness of tone (the dialogue is in effect the report of a drinking party conversation), Plato's main task is to determine the nature of love and, as its proper object, beauty.

The conception that Socrates advances of love is that it is what mediates between the temporal and the eternal realms: love is the path through which mortal man can come to enter the sphere of higher, universal truth. Setting aside the somewhat problematic metaphysical aspect of this, the idea of love that emerges is defined by its mediatory role: love is the form taken by our encounter with ultimate truth, a truth which for Socrates and his apologist Plato is one and the same as moral goodness. The idea of beauty, in turn, is conceived as the proper object of our love. Constitutionally, we are bound to love that which is beautiful. The theory that Socrates proposes is that our awareness of beauty exists on a relational scale – referred to as a 'ladder' in the text – according to which, having come to know the lower beauties such as those of the appearance of things and people, we move up the ladder, coming to understand first the beauty of art, then the higher beauties of human intelligence and, finally, the divine source of the good.

The importance of this account, for our purposes, is not the metaphysical structure that Plato invokes of lower and higher realities. Rather, it is the intrinsic connection between beauty and goodness that he posits, and the fact that our experience of beauty – which is also, by definition, an experience of loving – leads us to the contemplation of things in their full depth. We do not come into contact with beauty, in other words, and leave it at that. Rather, the experience drives us to enter into the matter further. In this sense, therefore, the value of our specifically aesthetic experience of the external beauty of things and people, and of art, is of leading the mind to a higher plane. The value of art, in other words, is that it channels our desire for beauty towards a desire for knowledge of the good.

The implicit connection between beauty and goodness is not questioned by Plato because beauty is defined as the proper object of human desire, and this object is defined in turn in terms of goodness. The circularity of this co-definition is undoubtedly problematic. It makes no allowance, for example, for the problem of art's moral content, nor does Plato offer a theory that is designed to address such problems. The underlying structure of the analysis, however, is valuable for us in its presentation of an understanding of beauty as that which leads us on to develop a deeper encounter with things, and also in its relevance for our moral relations with others. For if, in coming to know someone fully – in coming to grasp their essence or soul, as Plato would put it – we continue to feel love for them, then our love is directed towards the beauty not of their appearance but of their soul, which translates as admiration for their moral character.

Again, an acceptance of Plato's position here is not without its problems, regardless of whether we accept his rather inflexible metaphysics of appearance and essence. Nonetheless, the idea that love, a specifically moral emotion, has the specifically aesthetic phenomenon of beauty as its proper object is both fruitful and far-reaching, as is the idea that our engagement with beauty is part of what drives and directs our continuing search for a truth which, at bottom, for Plato and many other philosophers, is best understood in moral terms.

A more recent investigation into this area has been conducted by the Scottish philosopher and contemporary of Hume, Thomas Reid. The starting-point for Reid's enquiry into beauty and goodness is, just like Plato's, the notion of love. Love, according to

Reid, is the sentiment inspired by beautiful objects.[1] In the eight of his *Essays on the Intellectual Powers of Man*, Reid argues that since the only thing we truly love is the good, the qualities that properly inspire love must be perfections or excellences of some kind. The beauty of objects thus has its ground in whatever perfections properly inspire our love for them, and, similarly, the beauty of minds are in turn founded in the perfections that inspire our love for them. According to Reid, there are three kinds of perfection that inspire our love of beautiful minds: first, the amiable moral virtues (such as innocence, gentleness, condescension and humanity); second, the amiable intellectual talents (such as knowledge, wit, humour, good taste, excellence in the fine arts); and third, certain perfections pertaining to the mind's active powers (such as health and strength).[2] Reid writes:

> Is not power in its nature more excellent than weakness; knowledge than ignorance; wisdom than folly; fortitude than pusillanimity? . . . Let us suppose, if possible, a being so constituted, as to have a high respect for ignorance, weakness, and folly; to venerate cowardice, malice, and envy, and to hold the contrary qualities in contempt . . . Could we believe such a constitution to be anything else than madness and delirium? (1969: 770)

The principal point here, then, is that we love beautiful minds precisely because they are of necessity wise, clever and virtuous. To use Reid's own words, '[t]here is therefore a real intrinsic excellence in some qualities of mind, as in power, knowledge, wisdom, virtue, magnanimity' and a mind in possession of such qualities is thereby really beautiful (1969: 771). On Reid's account, therefore, beauty of the soul and virtuous character coincide because to be genuinely beautiful, a mind must be virtuous. For it to fail in this respect, or for our initial conception of a mind's beauty to happen to have been mistaken, is for it to cease to be beautiful.

As with Plato's account, the highest form of beauty for Reid is ultimately to be defined in moral terms: beauty of the soul consists, by definition, in the possession of virtue. In common with Plato, therefore, there is something of a discrepancy between the paradigm of moral beauty and our everyday experience of love, the emotion characterized by its being directed towards this quality. For although we may certainly assent in theory, and claim that we are constitutionally bound toward the admiration and love of that which is, by definition, admirable and loveable – namely, moral beauty – we must also remember that the idea of human love is also distinguished by a certain tolerance of imperfection. That is to say, in practice, in so far as we may love an individual for who they are, it is the case that more often than not we love them not in spite of but partly because of their failings. For it is usually the case that a person's failings are as much part of what makes them themselves as their virtues. Accepting a loved-one as 'human', one might say, is an essential part of what it is to love them.

Furthermore, it is far from clear in an aesthetic context that those objects we come to love the most are in fact always those we effectively find the most beautiful, or deem the most aesthetically valuable. With art, as with love and friendship, acquaintance over time breeds affection. So, in addition to falling foul of the problem of Immoralism discussed in Chapter 5, it seems that Reid's conception of moral beauty also runs aground on the much simpler and much more common problem of perceived imperfections in those characters of people we love.

The most recent substantial defence of the idea of the beauty of the soul and the concomitant aesthetics of virtue comes from Colin McGinn. Profoundly inspired by Reid, McGinn's main claim, as propounded in his essay 'Beauty of the Soul', is the thesis 'that virtue coincides with beauty of soul and vice with ugliness of soul' (1997: 93). Adapting Reid's tenet that we can ascribe aesthetic qualities to moral character, McGinn argues that for a person to be virtuous is for her soul (that is to say, her personality or character) to have certain aesthetic qualities that are necessary and sufficient conditions for a person's moral goodness. To the question of whether beauty is thereby reducible to moral goodness, McGinn holds that although aesthetic and moral qualities are ontologically distinct, it is necessary to 'tie them conceptually together' (1997: 100). He is therefore concerned with what seems to be a looser connection between virtue and beauty than Plato and Reid, and is careful to stipulate that aesthetic qualities cannot simply be reduced to the moral qualities on which they are held to supervene. Nonetheless, the negative claim, to the effect that a person with a morally bad character cannot have a beautiful soul is upheld, as is the idea that a morally good person cannot possess an ugly soul. He expresses the matter most simply as follows: a 'soul' could not be 'both ugly and virtuous or beautiful and vicious' (1997: 100).

Although his language is rather different and, on an ontological and metaphysical level, his theory less ambitious, the substance of McGinn's theory centres on precisely the same claim as that made by Plato and Reid. Beauty, at bottom, is the image of moral goodness, such that, when we come to recognize this goodness for what it is – that is to say, when we become acquainted with the 'soul' of some person or thing – we cannot but find it beautiful. As with Plato and Reid's accounts, therefore, the essential idea is a very attractive one because of the strong conceptual tie it offers between beauty and goodness, a bond so strong in McGinn's case that the two come to be defined exclusively in terms of each other. However, to uphold such a strong link demands that we discount as irrelevant many of the instances of beauty that we subsequently discover to have no moral connection – on McGinn's account, such instances of beauty would be illusory or, as in Plato's conception of the ladder of beauty, simply things to have been passed through and discarded.

Perhaps more seriously, too, McGinn's account seems flawed in the purely moral case, independently of the relation to beauty. For whatever metaphysical apparatus we use to understand the concept of a soul, it seems highly problematic to assert that bad people are incapable of virtuous actions. Someone, for example, may have an 'ugly soul' in the sense of being consumed by hatred, jealousy and self-loathing and yet act consistently for the good of others in accordance with her better judgement. Indeed, on a smaller scale, such cases are far from being exceptional.

Ultimately, then, the idea of an aesthetic virtue theory, to the effect that our moral goals can be construed as aesthetically appealing in a way that is both consistent and capable of doing explanatory work seems somewhat far-fetched, despite the considerable appeal of its simplicity and normative strength. For the experience of beauty – and not merely transient beauty but beauty that is lasting and significant – seems to be far too common and widespread to assert that the concept of beauty is connected so absolutely to the concept of the good. The two may, in an evolutionary sense, be linked absolutely, but on the basis of our contemporary phenomenology and psychology, the divergence is apparent and, as such, must be accounted for. In other words, even if – perhaps in a manner that has been desired by a number of the philosophers and thinkers we have discussed – the conceptual and phenomenal coincidence of beauty and goodness is very much to be desired, such a situation remains a state of things to wish for rather than one to observe, strictly speaking.

As a philosophical theory aiming to provide not only a solid definition of the notions of beauty and moral goodness but also a satisfactory epistemological account of what it is to be an aesthetic and moral agent, the idea that beauty of the soul and virtuous character go hand in hand has relatively little mileage. However, to reject the proposal *qua* comprehensive theory of those aspects of value experience does not necessarily entail an outright denial of all that it suggests. First and foremost, we have seen that aesthetic experience may well, at least at times, serve as a kind of mental preparation or propaedeutic to the moral. Yet, and as Ronald Hepburn writes, that is not to say that:

> the aesthetic *must* or even *reliably does* bring the appreciator to the stance or attitude basic to morality: only that there is that important affinity between aesthetic and moral orientation. (2001: 58, original emphasis)

For it is perfectly possible to engage aesthetically with an object without showing the slightest interest in the moral character of that or a similar object. Moreover, and as Marcia Muelder Eaton has pointed out, 'in order to understand morality and thus become a mature moral person, one's action must have both appropriate style and content' and this, she continues, 'requires aesthetic skills' or a certain kind of proficiency with aesthetic concepts such as elegance and delicacy (1997: 361ff.). That is not to say, however, that if one fails to engage in aesthetic perception or assessment, it always follows from that that one is not a (good) moral agent.

What is more, even if the precise focus of appreciation is different in aesthetic and moral cases respectively, it is nonetheless true that cultivating our aesthetic sensibility, rather like our moral sensitivity, does involve becoming more attentive to individual details of a particular situation, or the specific needs and desires of other persons. In other words, we learn to perceive aspects of experience that a less perceptive or sensitive agent might not grasp.

Fundamentally, then, and despite all the similarities and analogies we have pointed out during our enquiry, there are still some important distinctions to be drawn between the aesthetic and the moral case at the level of agency. The claim that beauty and goodness are to be assimilated to one another, if only with regards to personal character, does not, in other words, contain the key to the best understanding of this aspect of the relation between Aesthetics and Morality.

USING IMAGINATION AND WEAVING A NARRATIVE

Of all the ordinary psychological abilities discussed in the previous chapter, one in particular deserves a little more attention in view of the special role it plays in both aesthetic and moral thought: the imagination. For, arguably, when we discern and assess value, the imagination is active not only in a purely projective manner but also in a more constructive fashion. On the one hand, the imagination operates indirectly at the level of perceiving aesthetic and moral qualities: it helps us see how some of a painting's (non-aesthetic) features render it sombre or lifeless, or grasp how a person's bare action gives expression to their vindictive spirit, for example. In short, it enables us to discern the various elements that we are given in an artwork and pick out which of those elements may yield the proper ascription of certain aesthetic qualities. For example, in the case of Picasso's *Crying Woman* the imagination scours the work for aesthetically salient characteristics that may, or may not, eventually lead us to describe that work as 'dynamic' or 'moving' or 'balanced'.

On the other hand, the imagination can be directly involved in aesthetic and moral assessment by construing an interpretative context in which those qualities are located and understood. That is to say, once the aesthetic qualities have been perceived and are 'up and running', so to speak, the imagination can create a narrative around the elements we are given which helps us to make sense of all of an artwork's aesthetically relevant features, and thus to make a judgement about its aesthetic value taken as a whole. This involvement of the imagination is important, then, because it leads us to experience the object of aesthetic appreciation appropriately.

Of these two roles for the imagination, the second kind seems particularly appealing to us in the present context since it is in this respect that the aesthetic and moral cases allow for the most interesting similarities and interactions. For in fulfilling this function, our imagination creates the broader structure within which the aesthetic and moral value of the object of appreciation can take shape – the framework in which the aesthetic and moral character can be understood in terms of its rightful interpretative story. Whereas the first form of involvement thus amounts to a kind of preparation for aesthetic perception and experience, the latter contributes to giving that experience its own life. To express the matter differently, whereas the first describes the imagination as it surveys an artwork and its potentially aesthetically relevant features, the second develops the larger picture in which we can assess and judge that work's overall aesthetic character. As Marcia Muelder Eaton sees it, aesthetics 'can become as important as ethics not because making an ethical decision is like choosing wallpaper, but because it is like choosing one story over another' (1997: 362). In other words, the way we employ the imagination in an aesthetic context may well be crucial to our abilities as a moral agent.

In moral deliberation, we employ our imagination to create scenarios that enable us to investigate the various courses of action and decisions available to us. As Mark Johnson has pointed out, '[a]cting morally requires acts of imaginative exploration of possibilities open to us in morally problematic situations' (1993: 131). We need, in other words, to build up narratives through which we can envisage the possible outcomes and consequences of a range of actions and decisions before settling on any particular one. So, in advance of making one's mind up about what to say, how to proceed, or which choice to make in a moral situation, we need to conjure up imaginative settings in which these various possibilities are acted out since so doing can help us see which action or decision leads to the best result.[3]

Somewhat similarly, evaluating a work's overall aesthetic character often involves creating a narrative, perhaps even a plot or storyline, which gives the aesthetic qualities a context in which they can be compared and possibly ranked. For example, assessing the aesthetic value of a painting such as Francis Bacon's *Person Writing Reflected in Mirror* calls for an imaginative act in which we weave a narrative structure that enables us to measure aesthetic qualities such as harmony, gloominess, serenity, unity and being lacklustre against one another. This, in turn, can help us get a grasp on whether any one quality overrules or should be emphasized above some other and which leaves a greater mark on the overall character of the object of aesthetic appreciation. By imagining the scene as though it were real and by puzzling together the various pieces of information available to us through the work, we can thus get a handle on the artwork as a whole – *qua* aesthetic unit – and so make a judgement about its overall aesthetic value.

While employing our imagination by weaving a narrative is fundamental to the final stage of aesthetic and moral assessment and evaluation, it is also highly relevant to other epistemological and psychological issues raised by the relation between beauty and goodness. For one, the imagination is involved in the continuous cultivation and sophistication of our aesthetic and moral sensibility. That is to say, in addition to predicting possible future events or creating imaginative contexts in the manner described above, the imagination can also be of assistance in visualizing the skills or personality traits one may want to develop or refine. The imagination can thus also help us realize our goals and aspirations as aesthetic or moral agents by constructing stories in which we act in a certain capacity or in a specific aesthetic or moral environment we find desirable.

For our purposes, it can remain an open question whether there are two distinct kinds of imagination active here (namely, aesthetic imagination on the one hand and moral imagination on the other), or whether there is only one imagination which takes two different expressions according to context. Nor is there any particular need to establish with certainty whether aesthetic imagination, if indeed there is such a thing, is more perceptual or propositional in content.[4] What must be pointed out, however, is that the role played by the imagination in aesthetic perception and cognition indicates that aesthetic sensibility is far from being either a purely perceptual or a merely affective kind of ability. For if we construct stories and narrative structures in aesthetic experience, then there is at least one significant sense in which aesthetic perceptiveness and sensitivity is bound to involve some more rational and cognitive elements. Aesthetic sensibility thus involves many forms of skill ranging from the more emotional and sensory to the distinctly cognitive. This combination, as we shall shortly see, is actually a prerequisite for the idea that being a good aesthetic agent goes hand in hand with virtuous character.

The experience of beauty, as we have seen, engages the imagination in such a way as to pull together actively the strands of a work into a coherent aesthetic entity. An important feature of this is the element of lived, personal experience: in discerning this kind of extended aesthetic quality of an object or entity, we do not simply 'see' the work immediately, in the sense of taking in the whole with a single breath. Rather, we actively piece it together on the basis of our thought, comparison and judgement. Similarly, our assessment of a scenario's moral character would seem to demand this lived experience in much the same way. Were our moral life simply to be identified with a discreet and fully worked-out set of moral propositions, against which we could immediately assess any given situation, the matter might stand differently. In life as it is lived, however, moral deliberation is precisely that: we deliberate because we do not immediately 'see' the right course of action. Not only is our ability to sympathize with others dependent on our imagination (for we must imagine ourselves in their place), but so too is our ability to bring to this sympathetic imagining the range of comparable narratives and scenarios that we require if we are to investigate a moral situation in its full depth. Without imagination, one might conclude, our moral faculties would most probably be stunted beyond recognition.

If the element of actively imagining the implications, resonances and deeper structure of a work of art is germane to our aesthetic experience of it, then it seems plausible at least that it is this element that comes into play during our moral engagement with the world. In other words, it is the aesthetic, or lived and felt, aspect of our engagement with the real world – an engagement which is nurtured and perfected through our experience of art and nature – that keeps the genuinely moral aspect of our deliberations alive, preventing our moral life from collapsing into a set of ready-made propositions and decisions.

CONCLUSIONS

It is in relation to this idea of the aesthetic and moral imagination as something that is not only fine-tuned and enhanced by the aesthetic experience of art, but which may also for some operations be entirely dependent on it, that we may most profitably return to the idea at the heart of Kant's understanding of beauty as the symbol of morality. For it is perhaps in this connection that Kant's notion of the free play of imagination and understanding – and its symbolic and sensory association with human, moral freedom – may be best understood. Such a 'free play' is, as we saw in Chapter 6, by definition a deferral of the moment of mental closure in terms of application conditions characteristic of a determinate judgement. That is, after all, precisely what distinguishes aesthetic judgement for Kant from other more explicitly cognitive forms of judgement. The importance of the aesthetic, in this sense, seems to consist in the way it keeps our minds open, so to speak, in prompting us to bring our imagination into play in considering the objects and situations that confront us.

From here, it seems almost a question of taste as to whether we want to embrace a fully-fledged metaphysics, such as Plato's, in which the ultimate constitution of the good is such that it is bound to appear beautiful; or whether we pursue a more pragmatic route, in which the apparent absence of any such neatly tied-up metaphysical and epistemological relations is taken as a simple reflection of the complexity and variety of life as it is lived. It should be clear, though, that our engagement with art and with the aesthetic sphere permits of moral extensions and incursions that are neither restricted in scope nor exceptional in kind; and that, further, these extensions into the moral domain in no way compromise or damage the aesthetic character of the original experience. For although it may be desirable if not ultimately confirmable to state, with Wittgenstein, that 'Aesthetics and Ethics are one and the same', it is nonetheless clear that it is beneficial to our understanding of both that the significant metaphysical and epistemological ground that they share be explored with a rigour appropriate to the philosophy of that which is most distinctively human in its scope: the idea of value itself.

NOTES

CHAPTER 1

1 It is not my purpose here to investigate this statement against the background of Wittgenstein's conception of Aesthetics and Ethics, but more generally to use his provocative formulation as the starting point for a more general enquiry. For more on the particulars of Wittgenstein's claim, see Collinson (1985).

2 See primarily Ayer (1936) and Mackie (1977).

3 For more on this topic, see Schaper (1968).

4 Although the term 'aesthetics' is derived from the Greek *aesthesis*, which refers to sensory perception, the idea of Aesthetics as a distinct area of philosophical enquiry dates only from the mid-eighteenth century, when the expression was coined by Alexander Baumgarten in 1750. For more on this point, see Baumgarten (1961).

5 See, for example, Dickie (1964).

6 An account along these lines has been defended with regard to artworks by Carroll (2000).

7 See, for example, Savile (1988).

8 See, for example, Berleant (1993).

CHAPTER 2

1 For more on some questions derived from this diversity that are not discussed here, see Sibley (2001b).

2 For more on why we value art, see Davies (2006).

3 For more on this topic, see Walton (1990).

4 Doubtless there are more, but these are the kinds of value that are intended and appealed to most frequently in the case of art.

5 Of course, cave paintings and rock carvings do not uncontroversially qualify as artworks in the first place. For that reason, it is more helpful to think of such instances as objects of artistic appreciation. For more on this topic, see Heyd and Clegg (2005).

6 The Conceptual Art made during the late 1960s and early 1970s represents the obvious exception to this claim.

7   For more on the distinction between intrinsic and extrinsic value in relation to art, see Beardsley (1965).

8   See Tolstoy (1930).

9   It should be noted that it is not because the *experience* of some thing is intrinsically valuable that that *thing* is itself intrinsically valuable. For more on this point, see Davies (2006), especially Chapter 6.

CHAPTER 3

1   See for example Collingwood (1958) and Tolstoy (1930).

2   For more on this point, see Young (2001).

CHAPTER 4

1   For more on why one ought to reject Radical Autonomism, see John (2005) who examines the suggestion that the artworks that we tend to value most highly are the ones that are in sympathy with our moral views.

2   See Kieran (1996), and, further, Kivy (1997).

3   For more on this point, see Moran (1994).

4   For more on this point, see Carroll (1998b; 2000).

5   For more arguments for Ethicism, see Gaut (1998: 189–92).

6   See Hanson (1998), Jacobson (1997), John (2005), Kieran (2001b; 2003a).

CHAPTER 5

1   Importantly, there is a distinction to be drawn here between erotic art on the one hand, and pornographic art on the other hand. For more on why pornographic art cannot be art, see Levinson (1999).

2   It should be noted that Carroll's argument explicitly applies only to the literary arts.

3   For more on this point, see Jacobson (1997).

4   See, for example, Kieran (2003a: 63–7).

5   For more on this point, see Mothersill (2003).

6   See Kieran 2003b for a discussion of the view that it is important to understand the sources and meaning of immoral views, actions and dispositions in order to achieve full understanding and appreciation of moral goodness.

7   See Hanson (1998: 206).

8   For more on the disagreement with Danto on this point, see Hanson (1998: 209ff.).

CHAPTER 6

1   For more on this and several closely related points, see Devereaux (1998).
2   These were, moreover, not to be separated for Socrates, for whom to be a good philosopher was to be a good person since philosophy for Socrates consisted first and foremost in attempting to answer the question of how to live well.
3   Another interesting text on this matter is Schiller's essay 'On Grace and Dignity' from 1793. See Schiller 2005.

CHAPTER 7

1   For an exploration of this idea, see Hutcheson (2004: 23ff.).
2   This is not to say, of course, that recommendations and reported judgements may not play a useful or even crucial role in drawing one's attentions to works, or to features of works; but, merely, that the judgement or perception must be founded on one's own personal experience.
3   For more on this point, see Sibley (2001a; 2001b).
4   See Kant (2000: §4; 211).
5   For more on this point, see both Broiles (1964) and Kivy (1975).
6   For more on this point, see Mueder Eaton (1997: 356).

CHAPTER 8

1   Interestingly, this contrasts with the affect properly inspired by sublime objects, which Reid identifies as admiration. It should be noted, however, that the understanding of the category of the sublime, and its relation to that of beauty, was undergoing constant change during the eighteenth century. Reid's use of the term is therefore not at all to be assumed to be similar to Kant's.
2   See Reid (1969: 792).
3   For more on this topic, see Lovibond (1983).
4   For more on aesthetic imagination, see, for example, Savile (2006).

BIBLIOGRAPHY

Anderson, J. and Dean, J. (1998), 'Moderate Autonomism'. *The British Journal of Aesthetics*, 38, 150–66.

Aquinas, T. (1997), *Basic Writings*. Pegis, Anton C. (ed.). Indianapolis: Hackett Publishing.

Aristotle (1986), *Poetics*. Halliwell, S. (trans.). London: Duckworth.

Ayer, A. J. (1936), *Language, Truth and Logic*. London: Victor Gollancz.

Baumgarten, A. (1961), *Aesthetica*. Hildesheim: G. Ohlms. First published 1750.

Beardsley, M. C. (1958), *Aesthetics*. New York: Harcourt, Brace & World.

—— (1965), 'Intrinsic Value'. *Philosophy and Phenomenological Research*, 26, 1–17.

—— (1969), 'Aesthetic Experience Regained'. *The Journal of Aesthetics and Art Criticism*, 28, 3–11.

—— (1982), *The Aesthetic Point of View*. Ithaca: Cornell University Press.

Bell, C. (1914), *Art*. London: Chatto & Windus.

Beardsmore, R. W. (1973), 'Learning from a Novel'. *Philosophy and the Arts: Royal Institute of Philosophy Lectures*. Vol. 6. London: Macmillan.

Berleant, A. (1993), 'The Aesthetics of Art and Nature'. In Kemal, S. and Gaskell, I. (eds), *Landscape, Natural Beauty, and the Arts*. Cambridge: Cambridge University Press, pp. 228–43.

Bermudez, J. and Gardner, S. (eds) (2003), *Art and Morality*. London: Routledge.

Broiles, R. D. (1964), 'Frank Sibley's "Aesthetic Concepts"'. *The Journal of Aesthetics and Art Criticism*, 23, 219–25.

Budd, M. (1995), *Values of Art*. London and Harmondsworth: Penguin.

Bullough, E. (1912), 'Psychical Distance as a Factor in Art and as an Aesthetic Principle'. *The British Journal of Psychology*, 5, 87–98.

Carroll, N. (1996), 'Moderate Moralism'. *The British Journal of Aesthetics*, 36, 223–37.

—— (1998a), 'Art, Narrative, and Moral Understanding'. In Levinson, J. (ed.), *Aesthetics and Ethics*. Cambridge: Cambridge University Press, pp. 126–60.

—— (1998b), 'Moderate Moralism versus Moderate Autonomism'. *The British Journal of Aesthetics*, 38, 419–24.

—— (2000), 'Art and Ethical Criticism: An Overview of Recent Directions of Research'. *Ethics*, 110, 350–87.

Cohen, T. (1973), 'Aesthetic/Non-aesthetic and the Concept of Taste: A Critique of Sibley's Position'. *Theoria*, 39, 113–52.

Collingwood, R. G. (1958), *The Principles of Art*. Oxford: Oxford University Press.

Collinson, D. (1985), '"Ethics and Aesthetics are One"'. *The British Journal of Aesthetics*, 25, 419–24.

Currie, G. (1998), 'Realism of Character and the Value of Fiction'. In Levinson, J. (ed.), *Aesthetics and Ethics*. Cambridge: Cambridge University Press, pp. 161–81.

Danto, A. C. (1981), *The Transfiguration of the Commonplace: A Philosophy of Art*. Cambridge, MA: Harvard University Press.

Davies, S. (2006), *The Philosophy of Art*. Oxford: Blackwell.

Devereaux, M. (1998), 'Beauty and Evil: The Case of Leni Riefenstahl's *Triumph of the Will*'. In Levinson, J. (ed.), *Aesthetics and Ethics*. Cambridge: Cambridge University Press, pp. 227–56.

Dickie, G. (1964), 'The Myth of the Aesthetic Attitude'. *American Philosophical Quarterly*, 1, 56–65.

Diffey, T. (1995), 'What Can We Learn from Art?' *Australasian Journal of Philosophy*, 73, 202–11.

Gaut, B. (1998), 'The Ethical Criticism of Art'. In Levinson, J. (ed.), *Aesthetics and Ethics*. Cambridge: Cambridge University Press, pp. 182–203.

—— (2003), 'Art and Knowledge'. In Levinson, J. (ed.), *The Oxford Handbook to Aesthetics*. Oxford: Oxford University Press, pp. 436–50.

—— (2005), 'The Cluster Account of Art Defended'. *The British Journal of Aesthetics*, 45, 273–88.

Gendler, T. S. (2000), 'The Puzzle of Imaginative Resistance'. *The Journal of Philosophy*, 97, 55–81.

Guyer, P. (1993), *Kant and the Experience of Freedom: Essays on Aesthetics and Morality*. New York: Cambridge University Press.

Hamilton, C. (2003), 'Art and Moral Education'. In Bermudez, J. L. and Gardner, S. (eds). *Art and Morality*. London: Routledge.

Hanson, K. (1998), 'How Bad Can Good Art Be?' In Levinson, J. (ed.), *Aesthetics and Ethics*. Cambridge: Cambridge University Press, pp. 204–26.

Harris, M. S. (1930), 'Beauty and the Good'. *Philosophical Review*, 39, 479–90.

Hepburn, R. W. (1966), 'Contemporary Aesthetics and the Neglect of Natural Beauty'. In Williams, B. and Montefiori, A. (eds), *British Analytical Philosophy*. London: Routledge & Kegan Paul, pp. 285–310.

—— (2001), *The Reach of the Aesthetic*. Aldershot: Ashgate.

Heyd, T. and Clegg, J. (eds) (2005), *Aesthetics and Rock Art*. Williston, VT: Ashgate.

Hospers, J. (1982), *Understanding the Arts.* Englewood Cliffs, NJ: Prentice Hall.

Hume, D. (1965), *Of the Standard of Taste and Other Essays.* Lenz, J. (ed.). Indianapolis: Bobbs-Merrill. First published 1757.

Hutcheson, F. (2004), *An Inquiry into the Original of Our Ideas of Beauty and Virtue.* Leihold, W. (ed.). Indianapolis: Liberty Fund. First published in 1725.

Jacobson, D. (1997), 'In Praise of Immoral Art'. *Philosophical Topics*, 25, 155–99.

—— (2005), 'Ethical Criticism and the Vice of Moderation'. In Kieran, M. and Lopes, D. (eds), *Knowing Art: Essays in Aesthetics and Epistemology.* Dordrecht: Kluwer, pp. 342–57.

John, E. (1998), 'Reading Fiction and Conceptual Knowledge: Philosophical Thought in Literary Context'. *The Journal of Aesthetics and Art Criticism*, 56, 331–48.

—— (2005), 'Artistic Value and Opportunistic Moralism'. In Kieran, M. and Lopes, D. (eds), *Knowing Art: Essays in Aesthetics and Epistemology.* Dordrecht: Kluwer, pp. 331–41.

Johnson, M. (1993), *Moral Imagination.* Chicago: University of Chicago Press.

Kant, I. (2000), *Critique of the Power of Judgment.* Guyer, P. and Wood, A. W. (eds). Matthews, E. (trans.). New York: Cambridge University Press.

Kieran, M. (1996), 'Art, Imagination, and the Cultivation of Morals'. *The Journal of Aesthetics and Art Criticism*, 54, 337–51.

—— (2001a), 'In Defense of the Ethical Evaluation of Narrative Art'. *The British Journal of Aesthetics*, 41, 26–38.

—— (2001b), 'Pornographic Art'. *Philosophy and Literature*, 25, 31–45.

—— (2003a), 'Forbidden Knowledge: The Challenge of Immoralism'. In Bermudez, J. and Gardner, S. (eds), *Art and Morality.* London: Routledge, pp. 56–73.

—— (2003b), 'Art and Morality'. In Levinson, J. (ed.), *The Oxford Handbook to Aesthetics.* Oxford: Oxford University Press, pp. 451–70.

Kivy, P. (1968), 'Aesthetic Aspects and Aesthetic Qualities'. *The Journal of Philosophy*, 64, 85–93.

—— (1975), 'What Makes "Aesthetic" Terms Aesthetic?' *Philosophy and Phenomenological Research*, 36, 197–211.

—— (1997), *Philosophies of Art: An Essay in Differences.* Cambridge: Cambridge University Press.

Lamarque, P. (1995), 'Tragedy and Moral Value'. *Australasian Journal of Philosophy*, 73, 239–49.

Levinson, J. (1999), 'Erotic Art'. In Craig, E. (ed.), *The Routledge Encyclopaedia of Philosophy.* London: Routledge, pp. 406–9.

Levinson, J. (ed.) (1998), *Aesthetics and Ethics*. Cambridge: Cambridge University Press.

—— (2003),*The Oxford Handbook of Aesthetics*. Oxford: Oxford University Press.

Lovibond, S. (1983), *Realism and Imagination in Ethics*. Minneapolis: University of Minnesota Press.

Mackie, J. L. (1977), *Ethics: Inventing Right and Wrong*. London and Harmondsworth: Penguin.

McGinn, C. (1997), *Ethics, Evil, and Fiction*. Oxford: Oxford University Press.

Moran, R. (1994), 'The Expression of Feeling in Imagination'. *Philosophical Review*, 103, 75–106.

Mothersill, M. (2003), 'Make-Believe Morality and Fictional Worlds'. In Bermudez, J. and Gardner, S. (eds), *Art and Morality*. London: Routledge, pp. 74–94.

Muelder Eaton, M. (1997), 'Aesthetics: The Mother of Ethics?'. *The Journal of Aesthetics and Art Criticism*, 55, 355–64.

—— (1999), 'The Mother Metaphor'. *The Journal of Aesthetics and Art Criticism*, 57, 365–6.

Murdoch, I. (1992), *Metaphysics as a Guide to Morals*. London: Chatto & Windus.

Novitz, D. (1987), *Knowledge, Fiction and Imagination*. Philadelphia: Temple University Press.

Nussbaum, M. (1990), *Love's Knowledge: Essays on Philosophy and Literature*. New York: Oxford University Press.

Plato (1998), *Symposium*. Waterfield, R. (trans.). Oxford: Oxford Paperbacks.

—— (2000), *Timaeus*. Zeyl, D. J. (trans. and intro.). Indianapolis: Hackett.

—— (2003), *Republic*. Lee, H. D. P. (trans.). London and Harmondsworth: Penguin.

—— (2005), *Phaedrus*. Rowe, C. (trans.). London and Harmondsworth: Penguin.

—— (2006), *Philebus*. Jowett, B. (trans.). Teddington, Middlesex: Echo Library.

Putnam, H. (1978), *Meaning and the Moral Sciences*. London: Routledge & Kegan Paul.

Reid, T. (1969), *Essays on the Intellectual Powers of Man*. Brody, B. A. (ed.). Cambridge: MIT Press. First published in 1785.

Robinson, J. (1995), 'L'Education Sentimentale'. *Australasian Journal of Philosophy*, 73, 212–26.

Rousseau, J.-J. (1965), *Politics and the Arts: Letter to D'Alembert on the Theatre*. Bloom, A. (trans.). Ithaca: Cornell University Press.

Savile, A. (1988), *The Test of Time*. Oxford: Clarendon Press.

—— (2006), 'Imagination and Aesthetic Value'. *The British Journal of Aesthetics*, 46, 248–58.

Schaper, E. (1968), *Prelude to Aesthetics.* London: George Allen and Unwin.

Schiller, F. (1993), *Letters On the Aesthetic Education of Man* in *Essays.* New York and London: Continuum. First published 1794–95.

—— (2005), 'On Grace and Dignity'. In Curran, J. and Fricker, C. (eds), *Schiller's On Grace and Dignity in its Cultural Context.* Rochester: Camden House. First published in 1793.

Shaftesbury, A. (2004), *Characteristics of Men, Manners, Opinions, Times.* Whitefish, MT: Kessinger Publishing. First published 1711.

Sibley, F. (2001a), 'Aesthetic Concepts'. In Benson, J., Redfern, B. and Roxbee Cox, J. (eds), *Frank Sibley: Approach to Aesthetics – Collected Papers.* Oxford: Clarendon Press, pp. 1–23. First published in *Philosophical Review*, 68 (1959), 421–50.

—— (2001b), 'Aesthetic and Non-Aesthetic'. In Benson, J., Redfern, B. and Roxbee Cox, J. (eds), *Frank Sibley: Approach to Aesthetics – Collected Papers.* Oxford: Clarendon Press, pp. 33–51. First published in *Philosophical Review*, 74 (1965), 135–59.

Stolnitz, J. (1960), *Aesthetics and the Philosophy of Art Criticism.* New York: Houghton Mifflin.

—— (1961), 'On the Origin of "Aesthetic Disinterestedness"'. *The Journal of Aesthetics and Art Criticism*, 20, 131–43.

—— (1992), 'On the Cognitive Triviality of Art'. *The British Journal of Aesthetics*, 32, 191–200.

Tanner, M. (1994), 'Morals in Fiction and Fictional Morality, II'. *Proceedings of the Aristotelian Society* Supplementary Volume 68, 51–66.

Tolstoy, L. (1930), *What is Art? and Essays on Art.* Maude, A. (trans.). London: Duckworth. First published 1898.

Walsh, D. (1969), *Literature and Knowledge.* Middletown, CN: Wesleyan University Press.

Walton, K. (1970), 'Categories of Art'. *Philosophical Review*, 79, 334–67.

—— (1990), *Mimesis as Make-Believe: On the Foundation of the Representational Arts.* Cambridge, MA: Harvard University Press.

—— (1994), 'Morals and Fiction and Fictional Morality, I'. *Proceedings of the Aristotelian Society* Supplementary Volume 68, 27–50.

Weitz, M. (1956), 'The Role of Theory in Aesthetics'. *The Journal of Aesthetics and Art Criticism*, 15, 27–35.

Wittgenstein, L. (1961), *Tractatus Logico-Philosophicus.* In Pears, D. F. and McGuinness, B. F. (trans.). London: Routledge & Kegan Paul.

—— (1984), *Notebooks 1914–1916.* Chicago: University of Chicago Press.

Young, J. O. (2001), *Art and Knowledge.* London: Routledge.

INDEX

Related Titles

continuum

ISBN	TITLE	AUTHOR
978-08264-7695-1	Anti-Oedipus	Deleuze, Gilles
978-08264-7694-4	A Thousand Plateaus	Deleuze, Gilles
978-08264-7691-3	Aesthetic Theory	Adorno, Theodor W.
978-08264-7791-0	Marx's Concept of Man	Fromm, Erich
978-08264-7704-0	The Essence of Truth	Heidegger, Martin
978-08264-7711-8	Positions	Derrida, Jacques
978-08264-7706-4	Cinema II	Deleuze, Gilles
978-08264-7705-7	Cinema I	Deleuze, Gilles
978-08264-7930-3	Francis Bacon	Deleuze, Gilles
978-08264-7929-7	Infinite Thought	Badiou, Alain
978-08264-7936-5	The Essence of Human Freedom	Heidegger, Martin
978-08264-9076-6	The Fold	Deleuze, Gilles
978-08264-9075-9	Nietzsche and Philosophy	Deleuze, Gilles
978-08264-9324-8	Theoretical Writings	Badiou, Alain
978-08264-9903-5	Beyond the Verse	Levinas, Emmanuel
978-08264-9904-2	In the Time of the Nations	Levinas, Emmanuel
978-08264-9960-8	Philosophy of Modern Music	Adorno, Theodor W.

ORDER NOW!

From your preferred bookseller

Or contact us at:
Tel +44 (0)1202 665 432
Email orders@orcabookservices.co.uk

www.continuumbooks.com